A GIFT FOR:

FROM:

This edition published in 2016 by Hallmark Gift
Books, a division of Hallmark Cards, Inc., Kansas
City, MO 64141 under license from HarperCollins
Publishers.
Visit us on the Web at Hallmark.com.

Editorial Director: Delia Berrigan
Editor: Kara Goodier
Art Director: Chris Opheim
Designer: Brian Pilachowski
Production Designer: Dan Horton

ISBN: 978-1-63059-965-2
BOK2256

Made in China
0117

HOW NOT To Act OLD

BY PAMELA REDMOND SATRAN

Hallmark

HARPER

INTRODUCTION

OK, so you go to the gym, but do you shred? You don't wear orthopedic shoes, but can you grind? You own a cell phone, but do you make calls with your index finger and leave voice mails?

If so, you may be acting older—a lot older—than you think you are.

I know, I know, you believed it would never happen to you. You thought you'd be cool forever. And then, seemingly overnight, the evil young changed all the rules and you're left feeling . . . well, definitely something other than awesome.

Don't worry. The point here isn't to act like a twenty-six-year-old, God forbid. It's just to learn how not to act like somebody a twenty-six-year-old might snicker at. Or, failing that, at least to know when you're doing or saying something that might be construed as a mite over the hill—even if you don't want to change it.

Fans of hownottoactold.com will find this book features two-thirds all-new material, information that's never appeared on the Web site. And fans of the book should check in regularly at the site to find up-to-the-minute bulletins on how to keep not acting ancient.

We may be older than them. And tireder, saggier, crankier, and more overwhelmed. We might be loathe to wax our nether regions or adopt the thong—but at least when we act old, we'll know we're doing it.

STOP USING E-MAIL

L eave it to the evil young to get all of us old people addicted to e-mail, and then to abandon the form in favor of texting and Facebook. Like bikini waxing (more on that later), e-mail is proving to be one of the Great Age Divides. Old people can't figure out why anyone would text, IM, or Facebook (wait: is that a verb?) instead of e-mail; How can you be articulate while typing with your thumbs? Why would you want everything you say to be public?

And young people hate e-mailing because it's . . . old.

Well, I don't care if e-mail is old; I can't stop using it. That's right, I'm addicted to e-mail, just as I am to dark chocolate after lunch and nitrous oxide at the dentist. I joined LinkedIn and Facebook and all those other services, and now I don't know what to do with them—or on them—or however you say it. So if you want to get in touch with me, send me an e-mail.

Just make sure it doesn't look like this one:

HOW NOT TO E-MAIL OLD: 10 MUSTS TO AVOID

July 12, 2016[1]
Dear Pam,[2]

Thank you for inviting me to your party.[3]

Unfortunately,[4] I will not be able to attend as I'll be having my false teeth fitted that day. My teeth have been bothering me for quite some time.

You know how it is when your gums start receding and then you crack a tooth or two chomping down on hard candy. Next thing you know you need a root canal, and then a crown, and then it's just a house of cards in there.[5]

That's what happened to me, and so I found this dentist, Dr. Marino, out in Clifton, who said he'd pull them all out for just $4,000, which sounded like a bargain to me, so I told him. . . .[6]

So write back and tell me what's going on with you.[7]

Your friend,[8]
Don[9]
www.donjenson.com[10]

[1]Redundant, since all e-mails are date-stamped.
[2]E-mails don't need a formal salutation, *à la* the letters you learned to write in fourth grade.
[3]Nice, but capitalization, full sentences, and formal statements like this just say old, old, old.
[4]Proper punctuation? Actual paragraphs? We don't think so.
[5]TMI! Don't you know e-mails are public documents?
[6]Zzzzzzz. This got way too long two paragraphs ago.
[7]Sure, and I'll send it via carrier pigeon.
[8]Not anymore.
[9]We know.
[10]Very gauche to include your own Web site. Better: barackobama.com or boston.com/bigpicture/, aka a site you love or a cause you believe in.

DON'T SAY "AWESOME," "DUDE," OR "YO, YOU COPPED FIRE, SON"

Slang is basically a shorthand way to let other people know how old you are. The problem is it doesn't work as simply and directly as you might think.

Using too-young slang, for instance, can very easily backfire and make you seem older, not younger, than you are. It's akin to wearing a yellow miniskirt or driving a Zipcar; you're trying too hard to be comfortable with something that was obviously minted by and for a generation that came way after yours.

The word *awesome* is a prime example. Few people over the age of forty can say "awesome" in what sounds like their native tongue. For the most part, if you're older than forty, don't even attempt to say anything more modern than "cool."

Of course, you also don't want to swing too far the other way and use outmoded words like keen, neat, or smart.

It goes without saying that you must avoid such adolescent and hipster lingo as *phat*, *fierce*, and *dope*. Even typing those words makes me feel a little sick, and I mean that in the old-fashioned, barfy sense of the word.

It may, however, be possible to successfully straddle the young-old slang divide and come up with something both cool and age-free by using outmoded words with confidence and irony. Groovy!

UNSTRAP THAT ROLEX

"What?" you ask. "What's the problem with my watch? Ohhhh, maybe it's that I'm not supposed to wear something so *expensive* strapped around my wrist. I guess that's the thing that makes me look old, bourgeois, and overly self-satisfied."

Well, yeah, except that's not really the problem. The problem is wearing any watch at all. The young do not wear watches. In fact, a naked wrist has become as emblematic of youth as ungray hair and a perky butt.

Young people use their cell phones to tell the time, and if you want to seem young, you should, too. Just remember to flip your phone open or light it up with one hand, and to use your thumb—not your index finger—to do whatever it is you need to do. And try to make out the numbers without having to put on your glasses.

AVOID DIRECT CONFRONTATION

Maybe it's this silent, desktop world we inhabit. Maybe it's the new culture of positivity and triumph over depression. But having a big confrontation, complete with shouting, threats, revelations, and tears is a decidedly old, out-of-it thing to do.

If young people want to fire you or stop seeing you, they'll just stop returning your messages. Or defriend you on Facebook. If they're angry about something you've done to them, they'll blog about it. Or send topless pictures of you on their cell phones to all their friends. I'm not kidding.

So what do you do if you have a problem with someone young? First, do some deep breathing, take a yoga class, drink a martini—whatever you need to do to get in a more, ahem, relaxed mood. Then, if you must raise the issue, do so electronically, couched in passive-aggressive—or even passive-passive—language. Say you're having some "issues" with the "process." Or rather, say "I'm wondering whether you're having an issue with our process?"

Question marks at the end of every sentence are good. Then, if the other person responds, don't reply. Or take at least twice as long to respond as he or she took in the first place. If you're as wise as you should be by your age, you'll learn to keep your mouth shut until the problem disappears by itself . . . or the offending young person moves to Seattle.

DON'T LEAVE A MESSAGE

This is a weird one, contributed by my nineteen-year-old son Joe. Only old people leave voice mails, says Joe. Young people, accustomed to communicating by cell phone rather than landline, figure that their missed connections will see their number in missed calls and return the call if they want or need to talk. Urgent message? Send a text.

Since discovering this tip, I and several other old people of my acquaintance have tried it with amazing results. Before, when I had something important to tell a student or an assistant or a child, I'd leave a long, detailed voice message on her cell phone . . . and would never get called back.

Then I tried leaving a short, detailed message: "Call me as soon as you get this."

Maybe three days later, I'd hear from her—when I'd forgotten why I had called in the first place.

Then I started using the magic technique. Say nothing. Just hang up. And like magic, the young people in my life started returning my calls instantly.

WHAT THIS TELLS US:

Unlike you, when a young person doesn't answer his cell phone, it's not because he a) didn't hear it, b) forgot to charge it, or c) left it in his other purse. When a young person doesn't answer his cell phone, it's because he saw your name and number on the screen and didn't want to talk to you.

If you leave a detailed message, she'll be so annoyed that she won't listen to the message, nor will she call you back because she'll be under the illusion that she's already talked to you—or, more precisely, that you've already talked to her.

If you say nothing, you'll be speaking his language. Plus, he'll get nervous that what you have to tell him is so bad or so good you couldn't leave it on voice mail. Plus, he'll be curious. And he'll call you back.

DON'T DANCE TO "SEXUAL HEALING"

8 BEST OLD PEOPLE SONGS TO DANCE TO . . .

If, like me, you can't stop dancing to old sexy songs, at least pick the right old sexy songs. Here are some great ones:

1. "Let's Get It On," Marvin Gaye
2. "Boogie Nights," Heatwave
3. "Love Train," The O'Jays
4. "(Love Is Like a) Heat Wave," Martha and the Vandellas
5. "Sex Machine," James Brown
6. "Billie Jean," Michael Jackson
7. "RESPECT," Aretha Franklin
8. "Night Fever," The Bee Gees

AND 7 YOUNG ONES THAT MAY ACTUALLY GET YOU GOING

1. "Don't Stop the Music," Rihanna
2. "Shake That Thing," Sean Paul
3. "Shake It Off," Taylor Swift
4. "Crazy in Love," Beyoncé
5. "D.A.N.C.E," Justice
6. "Yeah!" Usher
7. "Hot in Herre," Nelly

12 WAYS
NOT TO WORK OLD

Want to get and keep your job without being pegged old, aka tired and out-of-it? Here's how not to act old at work:

1. **Don't Arrive at the Crack of Dawn** and make everybody feel guilty for not being there as early as you. If you're bushy-tailed and at your desk by 6:35, at least have the good grace to keep your mouth shut about it.

2. **Don't Bring the Donuts.** You don't need to be Mommy or Daddy to the entire office, showing up with coffee, remembering all the birthdays, making sure everybody signs the card.

3. **Don't Punch the Clock.** Of course, you may have to punch an actual clock at your workplace, but we mean this more metaphorically. Don't treat your job like a prison where you're just putting in your time.

4. **Stifle the Self-Aggrandizing Anecdotes.** Reminiscing about the year you almost won the Pulitzer or that time you saved the company a million dollars won't convince people you're cooler than they already think you are.

5. **Don't Be Tough.** The young gestalt is much softer and less direct. People ask questions and seem to defer to others even when they have a strong opinion. And if they want to do it their way anyway, they'll just go ahead without discussion or confrontation.

6. **Keep It Zipped**—and I don't mean just your mouth. Don't think that just because you got the memo about sexual harassment that your behavior is squeaky clean. Making off-color jokes, talking about your personal life, asking your coworkers about last night's date, or commenting on someone's clothes or body is not only inappropriate but kind of gross. And girlfriends, don't think you're exempt here.

14

7. **No Sexist or Racist Jokes.** And that includes mild, veiled, or oh-so-ironic ones.

8. **Don't Stay Glued to Your Chair.** Rolling everywhere, avoiding getting up and walking across the room, and sitting there 'til your ass grows around the cushion is definitely acting old—and won't do much for the way you look, either.

9. **No Long-Range Planning.** Looking too far ahead, wanting firm commitments on times and places far (i.e., more than a day or two) into the future is definitely an old thing. If you simply must plan (I know I must), do it in secret and be flexible if things change.

10. **Don't Be a Human Archive.** There may be value in having someone at a company who can detail the résumés of everyone who has held a job there since 1981, who can remember what year manual typewriters were upgraded to electrics and when secretaries were replaced by voice mail. But there isn't much value in letting that person be you.

11. **No Brown-Bagging It.** Carrying your lunch to work in a little brown bag suggests that you a) have actual food in your house and b) care more about pinching a few pennies than you do about going out with your coworkers or eating something interesting—or even skipping lunch to maintain your boyish figure. Brown-bagging is for people old enough to have mortgages and kids' tuitions to worry about . . . which is why this is probably one HNTAO rule you'll delight in breaking.

12. **It's Not All about the Job.** Young people may work more hours and seem more tireless, but they're also into kayaking, hanging out with their dogs, playing bocce at the hipster bar, and meeting other attractive young people. Getting too excited about your work—or seeming excited about work to the exclusion of everything else—will make you seem old.

BEWARE THE ACCIDENTAL HOOKUP

Admit it: you don't really know what "hookup" (or "hook-up" or "hook up") means. Is it meeting for coffee? Kissing? Having sex? Watching television together? Getting engaged?

The point is that you should avoid using the term if you're not certain of its implications. As cool and casual as it may make you feel, it's probably best not to suggest to your boss that you hook up later on this evening. Maybe not smart to ask your teenager whether he hooked up with any of his friends last night. Might not be wise to say wistfully to your neighbor that you wish you could hook up more often.

So what does hookup mean? Anything and everything, apparently. Maybe if we get under the covers and turn out the lights for long enough, the phrase and all its implications will just go away.

WHAT EXACTLY IS A HOOKUP? A TEENAGER TELLS ALL . . . WELL, SOME

What is this "hookup" we've been hearing so much about? When you say that two people are "hooking up," what does that mean, exactly? To find out, we asked our resident teenager.

Old Person: What does "hookup" mean?

Teenager: I don't know. It could mean anything.

OP: Going to the movies? Meeting for coffee?

Teen (smirking): Not that.

OP: What then? Having sex?

Teen: Gross! Stop!

OP: So hooking up is not necessarily having sex?

Teen: No.

OP: So if I said to Dad, "Let's hook up later . . ."

Teen: No! You can't say that!

OP: Okaaaaaaaaaaay. So it might not always mean sex, but it always means something like sex.

Teen: Not necessarily.

OP: So can it mean dating?

Teen: Dating?

OP: I mean hanging out. Going out with someone.

Teen: Maybe.

OP: So have you ever hooked up with anyone?

Teen: Leave me alone!

7 WAYS NOT TO WEEKEND OLD

1. **Don't Go Home after Work on Friday.** Instead, head to the nearest bar with colleagues and slam back enough drinks to achieve oblivion.

2. **Don't Maintain Professional Distance between Yourself and That Hot Coworker.** Once oblivion has been achieved, you can retreat to a dark corner and "accidentally" start making out. You didn't plan it! Nothing really happened! On Monday you'll both act as though it were but a dimly remembered dream.

3. **Don't Bounce out of Bed on Saturday Morning.** Sleep late. Keep sleeping. Zzzzzzz. If it's before noon, you must stay horizontal.

4. **No Chores.** Forget any notion that weekends are for catching up on laundry, going to the grocery store, cleaning the bathroom, cooking for the week ahead, paying bills, or anything else "productive." Weekends are for playing video games, shooting hoops, doing sun salutations, shopping for shoes, or sleeping on the beach.

5. **Don't Stay Home on Saturday Night.** You don't want to be home in your sweatpants with your feet up, drinking a nice glass of Scotch, and watching the first season of *Mad Men*, do you? Shut up, you do not! No, you want to be wearing a sequined miniskirt and high-heeled sandals and going to a club! You want to be playing pool, slamming back Jell-O shots, and dancing to "My Chemical Romance"!

6. **Do Not Read the Sunday Paper.** As a journalist, this one physically pains me. But the fact is that while almost everybody over forty reads the Sunday paper as religiously as our parents went to church, most younger people don't bother, believing that if anything truly important happens, the universe will text them the news.

7. **Don't Cook Dinner for the Family.** Invite the grandparents, the aunt and uncle, and their kids over for Sunday dinner? Roast a chicken, bake some brownies, spend all day first getting the house ready for guests and then cleaning up after them? That's for people who believe in sacrificing themselves for worthless rituals. And you, well, you have better things to do—like eat the brownies.

DON'T GET TOO EXCITED ABOUT MONDAYS

Hello, my name is Pam, and I am a Monday Lover. It's not that I don't like weekends, exactly. But on the weekends I spend a lot of time doing all those household chores—laundry, grocery shopping, weeding—I don't have time to do during the week. My husband and kids are around, wanting to be cooked for, driven around, and sometimes even communed with.

And then on Monday morning, they all leave. I'm alone, free to work without distraction or interruption. I don't feel guilty about writing instead of going to the bookstore with my husband or making pasta for my son. And if I sometimes sneak out for lunch with a friend, it's nobody's business but my own.

But when I was young, weekends meant fun and freedom and sex, and Monday meant a return to drudgery and imprisonment in some dumb job. Would I go back to that time? No. I love loving Mondays. But I wouldn't mind loving Saturdays and Sundays a little bit more.

DON'T BE PROUD OF BEING BEFUDDLED BY TECHNOLOGY

Sure, it's baffling. Of course, the mushrooming parade of applications like Digg, Reddit, Facebook, LinkedIn, and Twitter is overwhelming. In fact, I sometimes suspect that half those things are not actually real but a plot by people under thirty-five to drive the rest of us insane.

But the important thing is not to admit how overwhelmed you are. "I don't understand why anyone would use Facebook instead of e-mail" or "We still don't know how to work the TiVo" are things you must not say out loud.

Above all, don't make a big public deal (ya know, like I am right now) of how clueless you are about using your computer as anything other than a glorified typewriter or working all those mysterious buttons on your TV.

Just quietly hire a fourteen-year-old boy as your tech consultant. Or act as if you're above the whole technology tsunami—you're so cool, you're unGoogleable!—rather than be swamped by it. Use it, or don't use it. But don't act like it's cute to be befuddled by it.

WEB DIRECTORY 102: 12 SITES YOU SHOULD KNOW

OK, we assume you've heard of the Internet. You've Googled, you've probably even YouTubed. But what about the next layer of Web use? Here, 12 sites that most young people know—and you should, too.

1. **Boing Boing:** boingboing.net is, according to technorati (more on that later), the world's most popular blog, full of tech tips, pop culture, and curiosities.
2. **BuzzFeed (buzzfeed.com):** social news and entertainment, along with "listicles" and quizzes on trending topics.
3. **Etsy (etsy.com):** a center for buying and selling handmade goods.

4. Imgur (imgur.com): a constant stream of user-uploaded images and stories.

5. Instagram (instagram.com): a hub for sharing pictures and videos highlighted by various filters and trending hashtags

6. Google Trends (google.com/trends): see the Top 100 searches right now.

7. Pinterest (pinterest.com): sort, save, and share favorite images and links by "pinning" them to personalized boards.

8. Spotify (spotify.com): love Marvin Gaye and The Band? Spotify will suggest some modern musicians you might also like, and let you build your own playlists to listen to them.

9. Technorati (technorati.com): lists which blogs and posts are getting how much attention when.

10. 10 x 10 (tenbyten.org): an ever-changing array of one hundred words and pictures that define the moment.

11. Twitter (twitter.com): provides minute-by-minute mini-updates on what you and many others are doing, thinking, seeing, or planning.

12. Yelp (yelp.com): a collection of user reviews of restaurants, shops, and services.

DON'T ADVISE PEOPLE TO CARRY AN UMBRELLA

Quit telling otherwise-competent adults to pack an umbrella, wear a sweater, or go to the bathroom before they leave. You don't need to be the world's mom, always know better than everyone else, or take control of every task, no matter how mundane.

But what if, without your direction, your husband goes to work without his wallet and your daughter wanders out in the snow in her T-shirt and everyone within your orbit constantly has to go to the bathroom when there is no bathroom around?

Well, maybe such desperate circumstances will teach them to take a little more responsibility for themselves. If they turn around and try to blame their oversight on you, shame on them. And with all the energy you'll save once you stop nannying the entire world, you can do something really productive, like find a way to reverse the aging process.

16 THINGS YOU NEVER NEED TO SAY TO ANOTHER ADULT

1. Bring some money along if you're going out.
2. Are you sure you're going to be warm enough in that?
3. Don't drink too much.
4. Say thank you.
5. Don't stay out too late.
6. Lock the car.
7. Are you comfortable in those shoes?
8. You'd better wear a hat.
9. Is that coat warm enough?
10. Did you have enough to eat?
11. Did you brush your teeth?
12. Maybe you want to comb your hair.
13. If you don't hurry up, you're going to be late.
14. Do you have something to read while you're waiting?
15. Are you sure you have everything you need?
16. Are you sure?

DON'T ADMIT YOU'RE CRAZY ABOUT SPRINGSTEEN

Dear Bruce: I'm so sorry. It kills me to say this. But I love you, and I know you'd want me to tell the truth as I see it deep in my heart. So as wonderful as you are, as much as I admire you, as much as I still love to dance and drive to your songs, I'm afraid that makes me seem old, at least in the eyes of the young.

It seems like just yesterday—though it was 1975—that I first saw you onstage in Milwaukee singing "Born to Run." You were so sexy; I went out with a guy in my writing class solely because he looked like you. Much more recently, I saw you shopping for earrings in Barney's with Patty, who was much more gorgeous in real life than in pictures. I thought you still looked pretty hot—though a little less hot than you looked in 1975.

I don't know what's wrong with the Evil Young. You are obviously one of the musical geniuses of our age, constantly innovating and reinventing yourself, and I would have thought that if there were any aging rocker that the young could respect, it would be you.

But no. Say you love Bruce Springsteen, and the Evil Young give you the kind of look that says, "Oh, you wear support hose rolled down below your knees? You boil your chicken because your teeth won't stand up to anything tougher? I think I'll just shove your shriveled old carcass into this here ditch."

The solution? Never, God forbid, stop listening to you, Bruce. Without you, how would we run, how we would dance, how, dear God, would we ever have sex? No, the solution is to just keep buying your music and listening to your songs in secret, hiding the evidence from our teenagers and junior colleagues, just like we did when we were in seventh grade and didn't want Mommy to know we were listening to Elvis.

DON'T BE THE RICKY

In many couples of whatever age, one person's the Lucy, and the other person is the Ricky. One person is the Homer, and the other is the Marge. One person is Han Solo, and the other is Princess Leia. One person acts young, in other words: wacky, fun-loving, charmingly irresponsible. And the other person gets stuck with acting old.

(For those of you born after 1980, think Gaby and Carlos. Or Paula and Simon. Or any of the contestants on *Project Runway* and Tim Gunn.)

How do you become the Ricky in your relationship? Here's how it starts: you want to take care of your Lucy. She makes you feel so important, so intelligent, so capable. And then, as time goes on, someone's got to pay the bills. Organize the taxes. Discipline the children. Excuse me a sec: WOULD YOU PUT AWAY THAT ICE CREAM BEFORE WE GET ANTS ALL OVER THE COUNTER?

Where was I? Oh, right: the next thing you know, you're the Ricky. You're yelling and screaming and cursing and threatening. You're managing the money and blowing your top when the credit card is maxed out and the cell phone bill is through the roof.

Meanwhile, your Lucy, your Homer, your Han is wandering around in a daze, buying yellow shoes and auditioning for Broadway shows and befriending wookies. So tell me, who do you want to be: the screaming check-writer or the starry-eyed, golden-footed wookie-lover?

NO LAME
PARENTING
ADVICE

We think, just because we've been through it all, that young parents want our advice about how to handle projectile vomiting, frozen-food-aisle temper tantrums, failing grades in history, and curfew violations.

Well, they don't. They don't want our suggestions that they pick a normal name like William instead of a weird one like Wylie or Wyoming. They don't want to hear that daycare doesn't work when your kid gets sick—and a kid in daycare gets sick all the time. They don't want us to tell them to be firmer about saying no, or softer on television habits, or more involved with their careers and spouses and less with parenting.

They don't want to know what we think because it's all going to be different for them. They'll never get fat or grow bored staying home with the baby, they'll never fight with their spouse in front of the kids or lose their temper or realize way too late that they made a child-rearing mistake. Their kids, unlike ours, will always want to go to school and do their homework, will never grow pimples or defriend them on Facebook. And if we do barge in and advise breastfeeding or public school or a generous allowance (or solid food, private school, and no allowance), we turn ourselves into the buttinsky grandparent, not only old but ignorant and interfering.

The solution? Zip it. Zip! Zip! It's not like keeping quiet will hurt you. And if everything really isn't different for them and they make lots of mistakes we might have saved them from, well, it just might be possible to get a certain pleasure from that, mightn't it?

19 THINGS NEVER TO SAY TO A YOUNG PARENT

1. Are you sure he's warm enough?
2. You named him *what*??
3. I think she's hungry.
4. Who do you leave him with when you go to work?
5. Maybe she should be wearing a hat.
6. Where is your husband?
7. Where is your wife?
8. Don't you worry that the dog might bite her?
9. Are those socks warm enough?
10. Is that stroller really comfortable?
11. I think . . . maybe . . . you need to change a diaper.
12. Wow, you look ready to pop!
13. When are you due? Whoops, I mean, you are pregnant, aren't you?
14. God, you look miserable.
15. God, I remember having little kids like that, and it was exhausting.
16. Are you ever going back to work?
17. So is this the last one?
18. How old are you now?
19. Once they're in school, then what?

DON'T BLOCK The AISLE

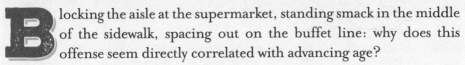

Blocking the aisle at the supermarket, standing smack in the middle of the sidewalk, spacing out on the buffet line: why does this offense seem directly correlated with advancing age?

Every time I find myself stuck behind some wide-hipped matron in the canned soup aisle, I experience a frisson of age-related fury. God, I find myself thinking, that person is so old and out of it. While look at young, energetic me, agilely maneuvering my cart around bulky displays, deftly plucking items from the highest and lowest shelves, efficiently carrying out my errands.

Whoops, sorry. Excuse me. I guess I must have been spacing out there for a minute, wondering exactly why I came down this aisle in the first place. Now I remember, I was looking for pancake mix, but I couldn't find it. Oh, duh, the big red and yellow box, right there in front of me. I guess I was so absorbed in trying to find it that I didn't hear you coming up behind me.

And then instantly I'm the old, out-of-it person who can't see or hear or move or think well enough to even be aware that I'm blocking the aisle. The cure? Online grocery shopping.

THROW OFF THE MIDDLE-AGED UNIFORM

When exactly did my town in suburban New Jersey decree that every woman over the age of forty had to chop off her hair, wash off her makeup, and start dressing in baggy black or beige linen or flannel, buttoned up to the neck, hanging down to the ground—and I'll have you wear flat, rubber-soled shoes with that, missy?

The middle-aged, suburban, woman-shrouding style is so ubiquitous that anyone wearing something bright, tight, or low-cut (usually that's me) is viewed with suspicion. What's she up to? Who does she think she is? Where is she going? And why is she flaunting it like that?

I say break out the hair dye, invest in some really expensive undergarments, and make your daughters take you shopping for once. If your husband feels threatened, if your friends think you're a traitor to the sisterhood, if the other moms question your fitness, let 'em. As long as you're still walking this earth, you might as well do it in shoes that click.

12 THINGS YOU CAN'T EVEN THINK ABOUT WEARING (FOR WOMEN)

1. Granny panties.
2. Granny glasses.
3. A slip.
4. Nude pantyhose.
5. "Dress" shoes with rubber soles.
6. "Dress" pants with an elastic waist.
7. Blue eyeshadow.
8. Dangly earrings with long hair and glasses.
9. Mom jeans: if they come from L.L.Bean, cover your belly button, and have a "relaxed" fit, they're off-limits.
10. A turquoise or lilac cotton sweater.
11. A flowered chiffon scarf.
12. A fake leather purse that's trying to pretend it's not fake.

As with everything, there are exceptions to these rules. But somehow, I'm guessing the items you own are not among them.

SHAVE THE SOUL PATCH

The age- and style-related migrations of men's facial hair remind me of the ups and downs of cars, say, or baby names. First young men adopt some facial hair configuration—moustaches, for example, or mutton-chop sideburns—that old men think is outrageous. But then, over time, the fashion migrates up the age ladder, until the only guys wearing moustaches are middle-aged cops. Eventually, after even the middle-aged cops decide that 'staches are uncool and shave them off, the evil young start growing them again.

Beards, goatees, and various lengths and shapes of sideburns have made this journey over the past several decades, and right now the soul patch, long the epitome of youthful edginess, has become the look of fortyish Web designers and hairdressers. Time to give the young back their hair patch.

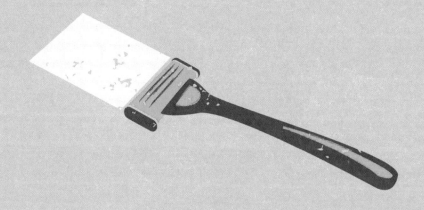

12 THINGS YOU CAN'T EVEN THINK ABOUT WEARING (FOR MEN)

1. Tighty-whities.
2. Undershirts under your shirts.
3. A turtleneck of any kind.
4. A suit, unless you're going to a job interview or a funeral.
5. A camel hair blazer.
6. Plaid anything, unless it's the shirt you bought in honor of Kurt Cobain.
7. Man jewelry. (Sorry, I have to take a hard line on this, but that's more my personal taste than any age-related prohibition. If your wife disagrees with me, you're allowed.)
8. A spandex swimsuit. Really: TMI.
9. Both halves of the pajamas.
10. Dad jeans. Just like Mom jeans: if they button around your waist, come from L.L. Bean, and have a relaxed fit, we don't care how cool you think you look—they're Dad jeans.
11. Sweater vests.
12. Square-toed brown shoes with rubber soles and decorative stitching just like the ones your dad wears.

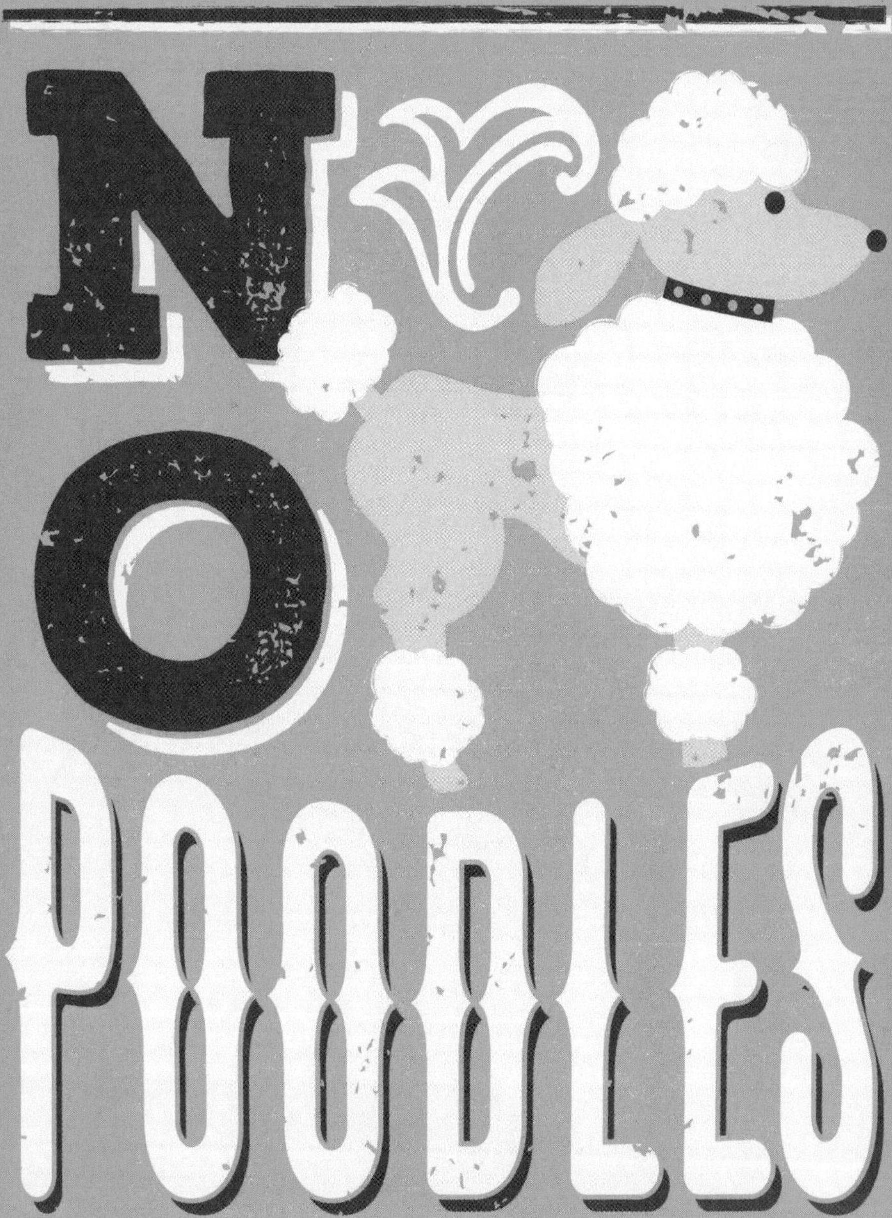
NO
POODLES

There are "young" dogs and there are "old" dogs, and I'm sorry, but poodles are owned mainly by people over forty. Why? Because they're practical: smart, hypoallergenic, nonshedding. And because they're out of style.

The small dog *du jour* is a Yorkie or a Dachshund, not a toy poodle. The big dog favored by hipsters might be a Labrador retriever, or even a Labradoodle, but never a standard poodle. The retro favorite breed could be a German shepherd, but won't be a poodle. In fact, poodles are so far out they may even be coming in. But owning one still won't do much for your Age Image.

PET MAKING YOU LOOK OLD? 5 SWAPS TO CONSIDER NOW

SWAP THIS OLD PET	FOR THIS YOUNG PET
Persian cat	Ocelot
Hamster	Rat
Donkey	Pony
Parakeet	Parrot
Goldfish	Piranha

DON'T YELL INTO YOUR CELL PHONE

Old people talk into their cell phones as if the phone was a tin can attached to a string, and the string was so long that the person with his ear pressed to the other tin can was in China.

Although cell phones are extremely tiny and not connected to any wires, they're really more efficient than that. You can speak in a normal voice—no, in a softer-than-normal voice—and the other person will hear you. We promise.

Sssssh. That's better.

8 WAYS NOT TO PHONE OLD

1. Don't be unable to find your cell phone because you put it away in a different place every time.

2. Don't hold your phone at arm's length—so you can read the numbers—and then dial very, very slowly with your index finger.

3. Don't be afraid of your phone: learn to program the speed dial, use the voice-activated and speed dialing, regulate the volume, even—wow!—use that tiny button on the side to flick off the ringer thing.

4. Don't be clueless about the other things besides making phone calls that your phone can do: texting, alarms, and . . . gee, that's as far as I've gotten.

5. If you've figured out texting, adopt a few of the basic shortcuts: idk ("I don't know"), yt ("you there?"), cu ("see you"), ttyl ("talk to you later").

6. Don't hurry off the phone because you're afraid of running up your bill. You have eight hundred minutes a month, and you've used only sixty-three.

7. Do not set your ringtone to the *Sex and the City* theme or the old phone tone (*brrring brrring*).

8. Try not to suffer from cell phone deafness, aka the inability to hear your cell phone ring or catch what the other person is saying unless you're in the equivalent of a sound-proof booth.

DON'T TALK ABOUT YOUR (GROWN-UP) CHILDREN

Going to parties where all my contemporaries spent their time talking about their grown-up children instead of themselves, the world, or, God forbid, asking about me was what gave me the idea for this book. It's not the fact of *having* grown-up kids that makes you seem old. And of course you can mention what they're up to if asked. But going on and on about what your grown-up kids are doing, where they're living, and who they're dating makes it seem as if they're the ones who are doing all the interesting things now, while you—you're past your prime.

Unless you're, say, ninety-seven or Jon Voight—make that ninety-seven *and* Jon Voight—you don't want to stand in the shadow of your child's life *or* use her glory to enhance your own.

Maybe you need to do some more interesting things. Or think of something interesting to say about the regular old things you're doing. Or simply recognize that, even if you're not that fascinating, I'd still rather hear about you than your twenty-three-year-old, whom I haven't even seen since she was eleven and frankly never found all that appealing.

5 THINGS TO TALK ABOUT INSTEAD OF YOUR KIDS

Perhaps you're so accustomed to talking about your grown-up kids at parties that you're afraid you won't have anything else to discuss. Here is a guide to some things to talk about besides your daughter's year abroad and your son's new house.

1. Instead of: "My daughter's getting married in September."
   Say: "Wow! Look at that hot guy over there!"

2. Instead of: "My son's deciding between Harvard, Princeton, and Yale."
   Say: "Don't you think this whole Ivy League obsession is a bore?"

3. Instead of: "My son is living in Japan."
   Say: "Been on any great trips lately?"

4. Instead of: "My daughter just got a big promotion. They love her, absolutely love her, at her company."
   Say: "I'm thinking about changing careers. What would you do if you could do it all over again?"

5. Instead of: "My daughter's about to have her first baby!"
   Say: "Don't you think sex is so much better now that you don't have to worry about getting pregnant?"

DON'T DRINK COSMOPOLITANS

Iknow they're delicious. I know they're fun. I know the "girls" in the *SATC* movie tried their darnedest to help revive the Cosmo trend they launched when they were in their thirties.

Martinis may be back. Sidecars and Negronis may be back. The friggin' Pegu Cocktail may even be back.

But Cosmos have become the official cocktail of menopausal women. If you're a huge fan of the Cosmo, you can youngify it somewhat by turning it into a frozen drink: fresh-squeezed lime, a splash of cranberry juice, a little simple syrup, lots of vodka, and ice in a blender. Mmmmm.

Or you could always knock back a Red Bull and Everclear. Or order a so-old-it's-young-again drink like a Manhattan or a Mint Julep. Or try one of these lethal-sounding young cocktail recipes:

3 YOUNG COCKTAIL RECIPES

1. Kamikaze

   Mix 2 oz. vodka, 1 oz. triple sec, and 1 oz. fresh lime juice. Shake all ingredients with ice and pour into old-fashioned glass with ice cubes.

3. Amaretto Sour

   Mix 2 oz. Amaretto, 1 oz. simple syrup, and 1 oz. fresh lemon juice. Shake all ingredients with ice and strain into a sugar-rimmed glass. May be blended with ice for frozen drink.

4. Irish Car Bomb

   Fill a shot glass with half Baileys Irish Cream (this goes on the bottom) and half Jameson Irish Whiskey. Pour a bottle of Guinness into a pint glass or beer mug until it's three-quarters full. Once the Guinness settles, drop the entire shot glass into the beer and chug. If you don't drink it fast enough, it will curdle and taste worse the longer you take to drink it.

LEARN TO TYPE WITH YOUR THUMBS

Classic old people behavior (of which I am guilty): dialing and typing on a phone with your index finger.

No no no no. You've got to pretend that your index finger doesn't even exist. Forget the middle, ring, and pinky fingers, too.

The young way to dial your phone or to text or type on your BlackBerry or iPhone is with your thumbs. Yes, *exclusively* with your thumbs.

There are online guides to thumb typing, but I'm too impatient, and probably even too old, to read past Step 2 in the directions. Instead, I've been entertaining myself by typing away as fast as I can (not fast) with my thumbs on my new iPhone (yes! I'm so cool!) and then chuckling over the mistakes I make and how the iPhone corrects them.

EDIT THE ANECDOTES

I was riding in the car with my in-laws the other day when we passed a little take-out place that specializes in Southern food: fried chicken, sweet potatoes, and cornbread.

"Oooh," said my mother-in-law, "Did we tell you about the time we went out to eat in Savannah and a storm blew out all the lights in the restaurant?"

Twenty minutes later, just as Mom was winding up this fascinating little story, we came to our destination and got out of the car, which reminded my father-in-law of the tale of buying his most recent Buick. And then, a bit after that, Mom told us the story about forgetting her tissues back at the house when she was packing her suitcase.

The point: The Greatest Generation is seriously attached to its anecdotes. Bring up any topic—dress shoes, say, or Coca-Cola, or the mating habits of bees—and your average septuagenarian will be reminded of a really great story that relates to it, however marginally.

The real point: edit your own compulsion to turn everything into a story. Sure, storytelling is the stuff of life. But anecdotes can easily start to sound like parables, which too often resemble sermons, which tend to put other people to sleep.

DON'T FEAR THE THONG

All right, you know you're not supposed to wear granny panties. But what's wrong with bikinis? Why does acting young have to mean wearing a thong?

Thongs are . . . uncomfortable. Even the ones that are supposed to be comfortable are uncomfortable. They make you feel like you have an intractable wedgie. Plus, they make you feel completely exposed—like you're hardly wearing any underwear at all.

But listen, that's the next step: going commando, *à la* Britney. So think of thong-wearing as a compromise in sexiness.

DON'T Lust After PAUL McCARTNEY

igh. I know, I know. I used to love Paul, too. I'd lay on my bed with the radio pressed to my ear, singing along to "I Want to Hold Your Hand." Wooo! I wrote Paul a letter trying to persuade him that the difference in our ages and circumstances wouldn't and shouldn't stand in the way of our love. And when Linda died, I was sad, but also, my heart rose in hope, just a little bit.

I still kinda think Paul is cute, jowls and all, but admitting you think so will get you branded as old. Why? Because, as my daughter says, Paul McCartney is "crusty." Ew. Some male movie stars—think Sean Connery—can hold on to their sex appeal seemingly forever, but poor Paul doesn't seem to be one of them.

But old guys aren't the only ones who can be crusty. Some younger guys can act or look like skeevy old ones and end up crusty, too. Here's the difference.

8 HOT VS. CRUSTY COMPARISONS

HOT	VS.	CRUSTY
Justin Timberlake		Paul McCartney
Jake Gyllenhaal		Ryan Philippe
Brad Pitt		Billy Bob Thornton
Will Smith		Willie Nelson
Laird Hamilton		David Hasselhoff
Mark Ruffalo		Marc Anthony
Clive Owen		Owen Wilson
George Clooney		George Bush

I'm sure you readers can think of female corollaries to this list, but I find it too depressing to do so myself.

NO CHRONIC HEALTH DISCUSSIONS

OK, if you're having a scary biopsy, or checking into the hospital, of course you should tell your family and closest friends. Yet as health issues multiply and other news in our lives recedes, it's too easy to tip over the line to Mabel and Ethel hunched in their rockers, one-upping each other on how many specialists they've seen, which symptoms they've suffered, and what gruesome tests and surgeries they've undergone.

See, even when you're old and sick and feel entitled to act like Mabel and Ethel, you shouldn't. So best practice reining it in now, before you start down that slippery slope. Can't order the cappuccino because you've recently figured out you're lactose intolerant? Just say "No thank you" and move on. Chest still smarting from a particularly aggressive mammogram? Wear a cozy sweater and suck it up.

No one wants to hear about your hernia, your endometrial biopsy, your colonoscopy prep, your polyps, your heel spurs, your Botox injections, your periodontal treatment, your nice young gastroenterologist, your implants, your rosacea, your collapsed thumb joint, your bursitis, your neck wattle, your reflux, or your constipation. Anything I haven't mentioned, we don't want to hear about that, either.

SCREW THE HOUSEWORK

You get married, you buy a house, you have kids, and even if you keep working, somehow it becomes all about the housework.

Here's what I mean: ask a fifty-two-year-old woman to describe her perfect man, and housework will creep into the description. He's great in bed, *and* he changes the sheets! He can cook you a great dinner, listen to you talk throughout the meal, *and* happily cleans up afterward. Come to think of it, we can do without the sex and the conversation as long as he does the housework.

Think of your ideal life, and again housework inserts itself. You'd love a big, gorgeous house that cleans itself! Cozy family dinners without the dirty dishes. A beautiful wardrobe without laundry. Great parties with none of the shopping, cooking, or post-party swabbing.

"Well, of course," I hear you saying. "We know all too well what it takes to run a home and a life. These things don't just happen; they take work, effort, and you know who ends up doing it all! Of course we want a guy who knows his way around a vacuum!"

Yes, but . . . you didn't feel this way when you were twenty-two. "I wish I had," I hear you thinking. No, you don't really wish you had. You wanted to have sex and fun and wear cute clothes and go to yoga and listen to music and have a cool job, and not only is that okay for twenty-two, but it might improve the view from fifty-two as well. The problem with housework is that it takes so much time and energy that you don't have anything left over for creativity and the life of the mind. You spend all those years keeping a perfect house because you think people are going to judge you by it, and then suddenly the kids are grown up and you downsize to a condo and you have no career and no hobbies and nothing interesting to talk about.

What? Oh, right. This is supposed to be funny. I nearly forgot.

MADLIBS: A YOUNG PERSON'S GUIDE TO HOUSEKEEPING

Old people make too big a deal of cleaning; it has to be done only every __number__ days. You don't really need any special equipment, just rags made from old __clothing__ and lots of hot __liquid__ in a big __container__. It's best to start in the __room__ which is usually the most __adjective__ room in the house. Get down on your __body part__ and begin to __verb__ the __noun__. Next, __verb__ the __noun__. If you want, you can listen to some __sound__ while you work or even ask __person__ to help you. You can use a __household appliance__ to get the job done more __adverb__. Don't worry if there are a couple of __plural noun__ left in the corners; it doesn't have to be perfect. As long as all the __plural noun__ are put away and the place smells like __fragrance__, you'll feel __emotion__. Pat yourself on the __body part__, sit back and put up your feet, and enjoy a new kind of clean.

STOP SURFING THE NET

If you still say you're "surfing" the "net," you've got to stop right now. I said RIGHT NOW! That phrase is just so 2003, or maybe 1998—I don't know, all those years pretty much run together.

Don't spend any time in "chat rooms," either. Or use the word "cyberspace," except ironically.

In fact, if you want to get all modern about it, what you should do instead of surf is Tweet. I signed up for Twitter, apparently, and I've gotten reports that a couple of people are "following" me, an activity whose dullness might be matched only by actually being me. What are you doing now? I'm typing. What are you doing now? I'm typing. What are you doing now? I'm still typing, dammit!

The real point, though, is that Web words have moved on.

24 WEB EXPRESSIONS YOU SHOULD KNOW NOW

1. Brain Fart: space out.
2. Cyber Monday: the Monday after Thanksgiving, aka the biggest online shopping day of the year.
3. Cyber Stalker: someone who stalks and harasses another person online.
4. Dead-Tree Version: paper edition of a newspaper or book.
5. Ego Surfing: Googling yourself.
6. Fat Finger: typo excuse.
7. Flame War: heated online exchange.
8. Geeking Out: getting over-involved in technology.
9. Impressions: number of times an online ad is seen.
10. Keyword: the word or phrase you use to search for something.
11. Link Farm: site that exists only to trade, sell, and publish links.

12. Meatloaf: unsolicited personal e-mail.
13. Mommy Save: saving a computer file without first choosing a folder or directory.
14. Patch: supplemental code that fixes bugs.
15. Radio Button: small clickable circle on a Web page.
16. Sandbox: limbo-like area to which new Web sites are consigned.
17. SEO (Search Engine Optimization): what Web sites do to try to come up higher on Google searches.
18. Texting Thumb: malady resulting from overuse of one's handheld device.
19. Troll: person who criticizes, baits, or attacks others online.
20. Tumblelog: a blog that's all pictures, links, quotes, and videos, but no actual blog.
21. Vampire Time: sleeping all day, staying up all night.
22. Voice Novel: endless voice mail.
23. Vubicle: cubicle with a view.
24. Widget: a graphic you put on your site containing HTML code that lets you access another Web site, database, or game.

HAVE NO PROBLEM

When someone thanks you, how do you respond?

No, not by saying, "You're welcome." That's not only old-fashioned but is seen by young people as faintly hostile, as in "You'd BETTER thank me, you selfish little snot-nose. Come to think of it, you should be licking my boots in gratitude."

And you thought you were just saying the words Grandma taught you were polite.

Neither should you respond, "My pleasure," even if you yourself find that phrase reassuring. It's also considered old-fashioned, and kind of servile, in the manner of your mom tripping all over herself to fix you your favorite snacks and do your laundry when you come to visit.

So what's left? "No problem." That's what the young say: "No problem." Or "No worries," or "No trouble."

Though to my aging ears, I detect a note of hostility in *that*. I mean, why would you say "No problem" unless there was the possibility of a problem in the first place? Sometimes, when I say thanks, it hasn't even vaguely occurred to me to worry about the favor that's been done for me—but if someone says, "No worries," I immediately worry, "Should I have been worried?"

Judging by how frequently they say it, though, young people have no "No problem" problem.

MOOCH OFF YOUR PARENTS

With more "kids" living longer than ever with their parents, why shouldn't you (in the interest of acting younger and dealing with the bad economy) join the trend? And it's not only a home you can mooch (or sponge, bum, leech, or scab) off Mom and Dad, but food, furniture, vacations, clothing, and actual cash money.

Some useful things you can do with your time and money once Mom and Dad are footing the bill:

Get an MFA in poetry, explaining to your parents that this will eventually lead to a lucrative career in teaching other people to write poetry.

Start a rock band, which will definitely make it big any day now.

Invest in Marc Jacobs clothing, which will make you look amazingly cool for two months—at which point you'll have to throw it all out and start over.

Become a rich and famous blogger, citing me as a role model.

If your parents are so elderly that they're dependent on you, then your only hope is to try to get adopted by some nice elderly couple who will allow you to mooch in exchange for watching *Jeopardy* with them while you eat dinner and getting up on the ladder to clean out the gutters because you know Dad can't do that anymore. However, as an older orphan I tried to get adopted once, and I'm sorry to tell you that it didn't work out.

What if your grown-up kids are already mooching off you? Here's the plan: you *all* move in with your parents. Then, late at night, when Josh and

Jess are out clubbing, and Mom and Dad are upstairs in a martini-and-Percocet-induced haze, you sneak out, run as fast and far as you can, and leave no forwarding address. There comes a time when even the hardest-core *moochacha* needs her independence.

7 WAYS NOT TO PARTY OLD

Not partying old doesn't mean you've got to regress to ordering a dozen pizzas and breaking out a keg. Just don't party ossified.

1. **Do Not Send "Save the Date" Cards.** That's like yelling "first shower" when you're still at the beach. Just because you show up with the invitation equivalent of an early bird special doesn't give you dibs on everybody's evening.

2. **No Pre-sunset Start Times.** Unless you're serving tea at a nursing home, don't start the festivities at four or five or even six in the evening.

3. **Don't Serve Expensive Beef and Cheap Chardonnay.** Old people usually get it the wrong way around: they spend days and weeks cooking the perfect food, then serve it with a couple of cheap bottles of warmish wine. The result: a bunch of people standing around feeling bloated, sluggish, and way too sober. A far better party formula is perfectly icy martinis made with superlative liquor and a dish of stale potato chips.

4. **Don't Spend a Week Polishing the House and No Time on Yourself.** Don't slave away making your house look perfect and then dash upstairs and devote five minutes to getting yourself ready right before the party starts. Get your nails done! Have your hair blown out! Take a nap, for God's sake! Once the room's crowded, people are going to pay a lot more attention to you than to whether your pillows are lined up neatly.

5. **No Bright Lights.** One of the top offenders at party of the old is glaring overhead lights—these not only expose every wrinkle but scream watch out! The grown-ups are here! Much better: candles everywhere.

6. **No Soft Music.** OK, everybody wants to talk. But haven't all these people been talking to each other about the same boring things for the past fifteen years? Mightn't they be ever so slightly relieved to find themselves drowned out by Marvin Gaye?

7. **Don't End the Party before It Really Starts.** Don't troll around with a huge black plastic bag in your hands, throwing out everybody's glasses and napkins when they've barely gotten started. Relax, enjoy your own drinks and food, spend time with your guests, and have at least as much fun as you want everyone else to have.

NIX ON THE NEGATIVITY

"It's all good," or so the young say. For you, that means you can never admit that sometimes it feels as if it's all bad, not even on the days when the sump pump backs up and the teenager comes home high and you notice your first gray pubic hair.

The sad truth is that life can be more and more negative as you get older. That's because our bodies are falling apart and our parents are dying and our friends are getting cancer and our kids don't want to be with us and we haven't had hot new I-forgot-it-could-feel-like-this sex for, oh, twenty-three years.

But who's complaining? Not you. If you have something bad to say—you know, any carping, complaining, criticizing—say it to another old person who speaks the same downer language. Or mutter it to yourself while shuffling along the street, poking at children and small animals with your cane.

Just don't say anything negative about, well, anything around a young person. If you're tempted to go to the dark side, simply say nothing, or consult this handy spin chart.

ANTINEGATIVITY SPIN CHART: 6 UPBEAT SUBSTITUTES

INSTEAD OF THIS NEGATIVE THING	SAY THIS POSITIVE THING
I'm so pissed they fired me from that stupid job.	I feel blessed to have time at home with my family.
My teenager is driving me crazy.	We think Ethan would have better opportunities at boarding school.
If I have to eat one more meal sitting silently across the table from my spouse, I will scream.	I'm spending evenings at the yoga studio these days.
It's so frigging hot/cold/ rainy/nasty outside.	I just love to chill in the house.
I loathe you.	You're amazing, and yet, I've been lucky enough to meet somebody even more amazing.
I hate my hips.	I love my kneecaps.

ENOUGH WITH THE MAN-BASHING

Sad, isn't it? I mean, there go half my jokes—along with nearly all my fun.

That's right; it's time to retire those quips about male refrigerator blindness and brains in penises. For those unregenerate man-bashers among you, there are plenty more great jokes out there.

But if you're determined to act younger, you should know that man-bashing has gone the way of bra-burning and do-it-yourself gynecology—just another relic of old-style feminism. Feminists today love men, appreciate men, even revel in gender differences without needing to feel that men are in any way inferior to women, a stance I wholeheartedly support.

At least that's my story, and I'm sticking to it.

DON'T FEAR THE SILENCE

Young people use silence to mean all kinds of things. I hate you, for instance. Or I'm not sure what to tell you, so I won't tell you anything. Or simply I'm busy, or I'm sleeping, or I'm distracted. It's hard to say, so I won't say anything.

If a young person important in your life—your adult child, say, or maybe your new boss—goes silent on you, try not to get nervous. Do not respond by chattering anxiously, leaving extended voice mails, or (the usual tactic of the old) sending several e-mails in a row. This will inevitably backfire, provoking even more silence.

Instead, chill. Wait 'til a text or e-mail comes in first, and then wait several hours—even overnight!—before responding. Make sure your reply contains fewer words than the original message: count if you have to. Don't get mad, just get silent.

What's that you say? This feels like high school? It's *all* high school, honey.

DON'T LIVE
IN WEST VIRGINIA
OR GREENWICH VILLAGE

Oldest state: Florida, right? Not quite. While Florida may have the highest proportion of people over sixty-five, according to census figures, the state with the oldest median age is West Virginia. Other states where the median age is at the top of the scale—over thirty-eight—are Florida, Maine, and Pennsylvania, according to the U.S. Census Bureau. Utah has the youngest median age—twenty-seven, the only state where it's under thirty—followed by Alaska and Texas.

Still, statistics are not what it's all about when it comes to not living someplace old. More important than reality is the *perception* of the place. Therefore, if you live in New Jersey or Connecticut, move to New York. If you live in New York, move to Brooklyn.

Places where young people flocked when you were young, like Greenwich Village or San Francisco, are likely to be young no longer. Why? Money, honey. Young people want to live where it's cool, but they have to live where it's cheap, which forces them to move to places that are less cool, which makes these places more cool, which makes them more expensive, whereupon all the young, cool, poor people are forced to move even further out to the frontiers of civilization.

Following this reasoning, Greenwich Village was last marginally affordable in the beatnik era, and now you need to be Graydon Carter to live there. Cool, maybe, but still old.

DON'T SAY
THE DOCTOR, THE COP, OR THE TEACHER
"LOOKS TWELVE"

I t's become a standard joke among old people to describe the authority figure they just encountered as being or looking twelve. Not eight. Not eighteen. Not thirty-two, which they (absurdly) figure is pretty close to their own advanced age, but eternally and inevitably twelve.

Besides losing its humorous edge, saying the doctor looks twelve really says that your point of reference has become alarmingly warped and you yourself look about a hundred and eight. Now *that's* funny.

CANCEL The DINNER PARTY

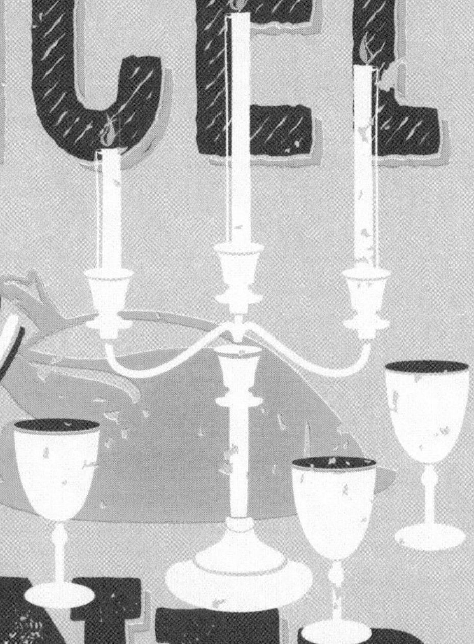

I didn't start throwing dinner parties until I was nearly forty. Too much work, too difficult to coordinate all those dishes—and who was going to take care of the kids while I shopped and cooked and cleaned and uncorked the wine and lit the candles and changed into a comfortable-yet-cleavage-baring dress and led the sparkling conversation?

And then, on our tenth wedding anniversary, I asked my husband what he'd change about me if he could, and he said he'd like it if I was able to give a nice dinner party. And so I learned. In fact, I got really good at it. Moving to the suburbs, living in a house with a real dining room, having more time on Saturday once our kids got older, we came to really enjoy dinner parties—giving as well as getting.

But now I think it's time to stop. I'm tired. Plus, they all start to feel the same. Now that I'm acting younger, I'm going to start inviting my friends over to share a keg and a bag of potato chips—if they're really lucky, a pot of chili—on Saturday nights.

7 WAYS NOT TO FACEBOOK OLD

OK, so maybe you think you're oh-so-cool because you're on Facebook. You've even located your wall, joined a group or two, and poked somebody. But if you're Facebooking old, you'd do better to stay home from the party. Here's what not to do on your friendly social network:

1. **No Formal Portraits.** Is your official Facebook picture the one your company's HR department keeps on file? Is it the headshot from your book jacket, or maybe your official wedding picture? Oops, sorry, using any kind of posed, professional picture as your main Facebook photo is old. Your Facebook picture should be slightly tilted, somewhat blurry, and should feature you smiling but not like you think anyone's watching, designed to make the rest of the world envious of how totally awesome life can be, but only for you.

2. **Stifle the Oh-So-Boring Status Updates.** Joan is making stew in the Crock-Pot. Steve is turning in early tonight. Ruth is stuck in traffic again. Can you hear me yawning from there? We all know life is made up of such mundane moments, but you don't have to tell the world about them every single time one occurs. Young status updates are ironic and cryptic. What can I say? The young are strange.

3. **On the Other Hand, Remember That the World Is Reading.** "Susan really doesn't want to go to her stupid job today" and "Dave just smoked a joint for the first time since college" are probably not messages you want to broadcast to everyone from the head of your L.A. office to your nephew in Colorado.

4. **Don't Friend Your Non-Friends.** Acquaintances, okay. Colleagues and neighbors, sure. Long-lost cousins if you dare. But it really is not cool to use Facebook to do serious social climbing or business networking by trying to connect with people who would never be

friends with you in real life. (And if you're on the receiving end, practice using that ignore button.)

5. **Know Where Your Wall Is.** Don't let your ignorance of the placement of various central Facebook features drag on.

6. **Quit Sending All Those Hugs and Trees.** Facebook has dozens of apps you can send around to your friends, to give them a little love today or help save the planet. These are infinitely dorky and annoying.

7. **Don't Be Insulted If—When—Your Kids Defriend You.** Now that the old are flocking to Facebook, the young are looking for another community, one with stronger gates. Until they defect *en masse*, recognize that ignoring your friend request or actively defriending you (you won't get a notice—you just won't be allowed onto their pages anymore) is not about you; it's about your age.

CRUMBLE THE DRIED FLOWERS

Nothing says you're desiccated like a bouquet of dried flowers—or five—arrayed about your living quarters. Dried flowers are the antimacassars, the china figurines of today. Doesn't matter whether they're hydrangeas from your own garden (you have a garden?), ornamental grasses you gathered yourself, or blossoms fashioned into swags and wreaths: dried flowers are the decorating accent of the middle-aged.

What kind of flowers should you display instead? Not, God forbid, plastic. Silk are nearly as bad. Even potted plants are a tad fiftyish.

Can fresh flowers ever be wrong? They can if you leave the baby's breath and florists' greenery in the arrangement. Or if the bouquet is turning brown or drooping: pathetically symbolic. But for the most part, okay, fresh flowers are lovely and ageless.

FORGET THE SIXTIES NOSTALGIA

So, you were at Woodstock? Ate mushrooms with Kesey, chanted with Ram Dass, wrote poetry naked with Ginsberg?

I'm sure that was all mind-blowingly groovy, but I have news for you, Grandpa (and Grandma): reminiscing about the sixties now is like recalling Prohibition was when we were young. Cue wavering voice: "Let me tell you, sonny, we got up to some crazy shenanigans in those speakeasies." For those of you who are mathematically challenged, it's been almost fifty years since 1969.

As further illustration of how long ago that all was, check out these words coined in 1929, forty years before 1969, from the Online Etymology Dictionary: beep, jeepers, deep six. But terms brought to you by 1969 don't sound much more modern: doo-wop, singles bar, and ego trip.

The point: the sixties are ancient history and not of great interest to anyone who wasn't actually there. So too the seventies: we really don't need to know who did what to whom that night you went to Plato's Retreat (ewwww, you did?) or what you snorted with whom at Studio 54. Even the eighties, which I basically missed thanks to the joys of parenthood, are getting kind of antique.

Young people are allowed to have nostalgia for the decades and icons of their childhoods: early Madonna and late Kurt Cobain, leg warmers and flannel shirts. You can reminisce about where you were in Y2K.

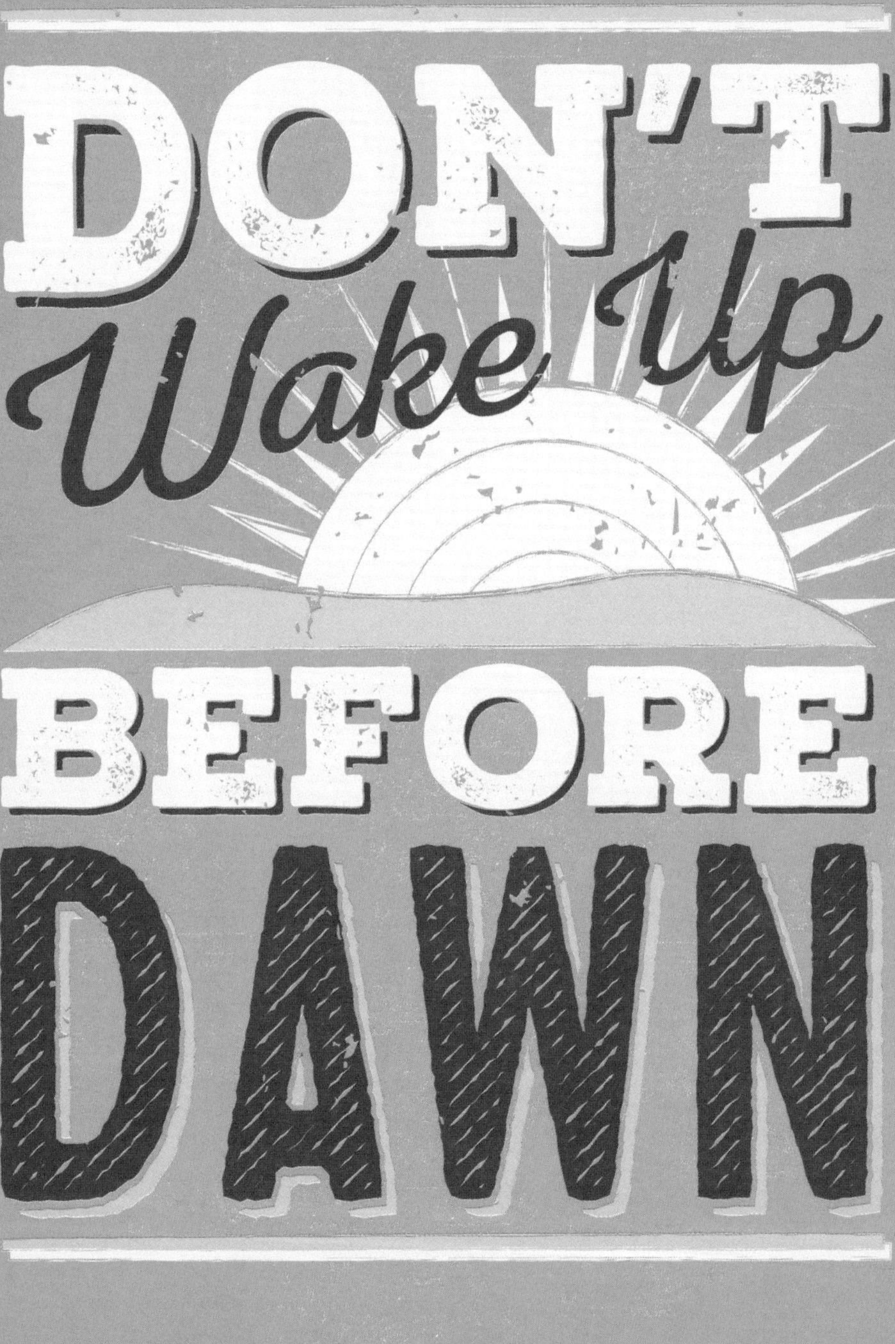
DON'T
Wake Up
BEFORE
DAWN

Getting up when it's still dark outside is what Seinfeld's parents did. Remember? Jerry goes to visit and is awakened in the dark to find his parents in the kitchen making coffee and squeezing juice. "We thought we'd let you sleep in," they say. To which he responds, aghast, "It's 5:30 in the morning!"

Ahem.

I was up at six today, Sunday morning. And that's after going to bed at almost eleven! Even when I stay up really late—'til midnight—I wake up at six.

I blame my children, for making me wake up at or before dawn for all those years to nurse them or watch cartoons with them or drive them to school. Now, although they ridicule me for waking up early, I can't stop. But at least I'm conscious enough to know it's an old people thing.

ENOUGH WITH THE JANE AUSTEN WORSHIP

I like Jane Austen as much as the next novel-writing and -reading middle-aged woman, which is to say a lot. Which is really to say way, way too much.

Do we actually need a whole genre of books about modern Jane Austen lovers, entire clothing lines devoted to Jane Austen gear, multiple tour companies eager to guide you through Jane Austen locales? How about lessons in how to take tea, dance, cook, garden, and, of course, write *à la* Jane Austen? There are Jane Austen Festivals and Jane Austen book groups, Jane Austen dolls and Jane Austen T-shirts, Jane Austen movies and Jane Austen bloggers.

Even our babies are not exempt from Jane's influence; the names Emma, Darcy, and, yes, Austen are rising in popularity. And once those little Austens get older, they can play with their very own Jane Austen action figures.

It's not that Jane hasn't written some great books, but there's something a little too order-seeking, rich-man-loving, and sanitized (i.e., fussily middle-aged) about the JA mania. Why not devote equal attention to the Brontës, who pulled back the curtain on a wilder brand of early womanhood? Or to modern masters of our own generation like Alice Munro or Louise Erdrich who are far less widely known and sell many fewer books than Jane Austen?

Listen, I love *Pride and Prejudice*, but I'd rather support contemporary female novelists whose talents are in more danger of being lost and forgotten.

15 COOL DEAD FAMOUS PEOPLE

1. Abraham Lincoln
2. Princess Diana
3. JFK Jr.
4. MLK Jr.
5. Heath Ledger
6. Miles Davis
7. Jimi Hendrix
8. Audrey Hepburn
9. John Lennon
10. Tupac Shakur
11. Amelia Earhart
12. Wolfgang Amadeus Mozart
13. James Dean
14. Coco Chanel
15. Kurt Cobain

8 UNCOOL DEAD FAMOUS PEOPLE

1. Richard Nixon
2. Madame Chiang Kai-Shek
3. John Wayne
4. Wicked Witch of the West
5. Jerry Falwell
6. Rudyard Kipling
7. Mata Hari
8. Lawrence Welk

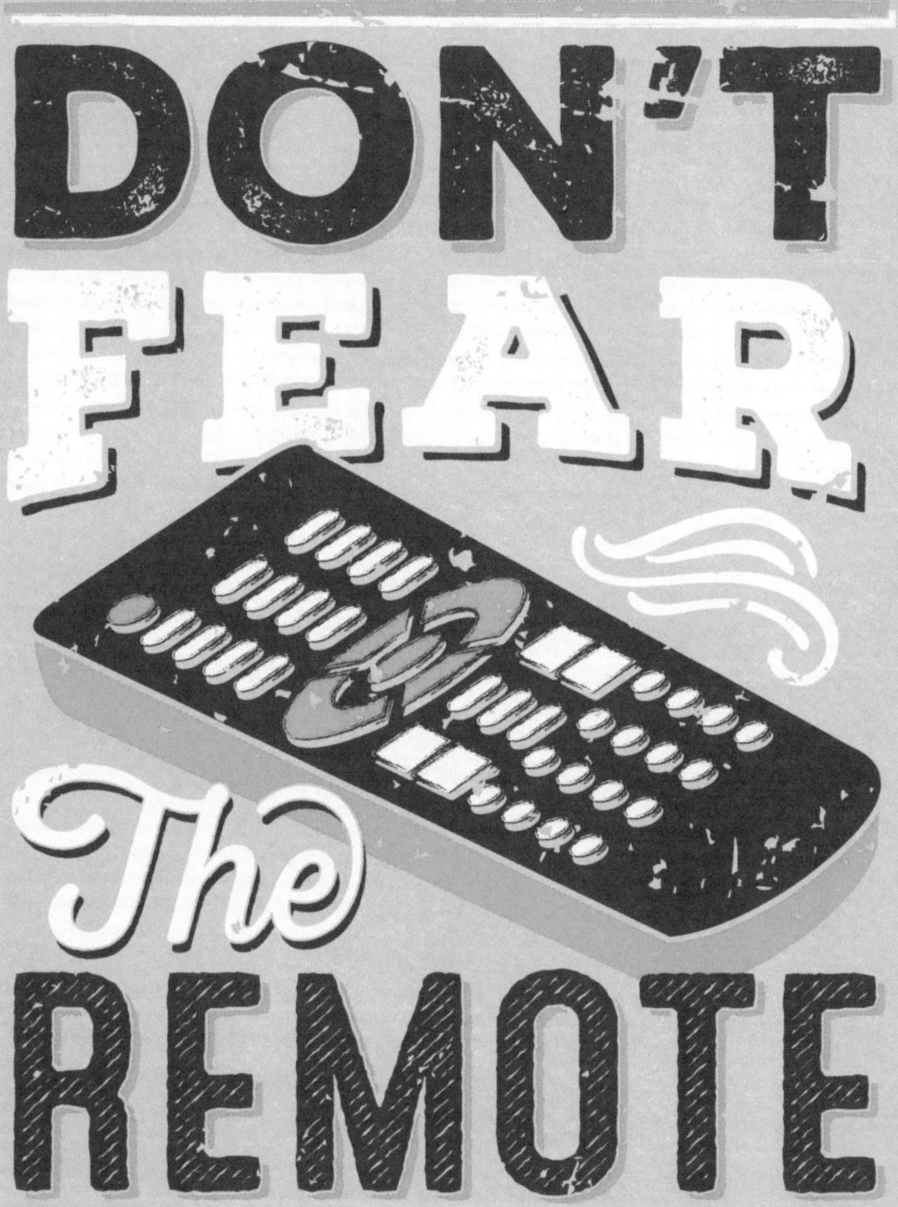
DON'T
FEAR
The
REMOTE

There's a moment in the life of all children when (if you and they are lucky) they leave you, not only physically but psychically—when their attention turns from you to the larger world, and when they become certain that they'll be happier seeking their fortune Out There than staying home with Mommy and Daddy.

That moment, for our older son, happened the night we called him at a party to help us change the channel on our TV. Until then, he'd always been around to work the remote, or we'd managed to muddle through without him. But that night we wanted to tune to On Demand, and no amount of fiddling could get us there, and so we finally broke down and interrupted Joe at his loud, beer-soaked soiree.

Right then and there, I think, Joe decided that he had to break free of the tyranny of our unreasonable requests or we would swallow him whole. And we found ourselves having to learn to work our own remote.

I'm not saying it's easy. Or that we've ever gotten very good at it. But we do now know when we need to be on CATV-2 instead of RGB-DTV and how to get there. We know how to TiVo one show and watch another. We're even capable of double-remoting ourselves from conventional to On Demand television.

Best of all, we no longer fear our remote. Instead, we fear our son.

NO HISTORY

History, don't you know, is for old people. If it happened before, say, 2001, who really cares? Nostalgia, revivals, historical tomes, national monuments, museums, antique stores, restored villages, and please, dear God, reenactments of any kind, just plain suck.

The reason history is for the old is that it makes them feel (erroneously) that there's something interesting and valuable about things that took place a long time ago, such as their lives. But there's not.

So let the old books crumble into dust. Tear up the mobcaps and throw the muskets in the fire. Ignore the historic marker, blow off the museum, and head to the bar.

If you want to not act old, you've got to live for today, forget the past, and believe—since you have no evidence to the contrary—that everything will be better tomorrow.

DON'T PLAN

When old people want to go on vacation to, say, Italy next summer, what do they do? They buy tickets. Book a hotel. Research restaurants and make reservations. They plan, in other words, just like they plan dinner parties for three weeks from Saturday, buy theater tickets for Thanksgiving, and make a mammogram appointment for the following April.

If you want not to act old, you've got to be a little looser than that—nay, a lot looser. Decide what you're going to do on the spur of the moment, depending on how you feel. Make travel arrangements on the fly. Throw out your calendars and datebooks. Be here now.

DON'T BE NAMED BOB OR PAT

O r Pam or, God forbid, Dick. There's a whole generation of names last popular in the forties and fifties—Karen and Donald, Barbara and Leonard—that you've got to avoid if you don't want to seem old.

Of course, you didn't choose your own name and you're pretty much stuck with it, unless you want to do something really radical and change it to one that sounds young: Josh or Jessica, if you want to go thirtyish. But those names are aging fast, so you may want to go even younger, with a name like Justice or Jagger. Or turn the whole age-name thing on its head and pick a really old name that's popular for babies: Matilda, say, or even Moses.

CHANGE YOUR NAME/CHANGE YOUR AGE: 10 UPDATES FOR YOUR OLD FART NAME

Use this handy chart to convert your old person's name to a younger model. For a subtle change, go slightly younger—or go all the way to childlike!

REGULAR OLD NAME	10 YEARS YOUNGER	30 YEARS YOUNGER
Judy	Jody	Jolie
Ken	Kent	Kendall
Mary	Mariah	Mackenzie
Wayne	Blaine	Zane
Carol	Holly	Christmas
Bill	Will	Willow
Kathy	Katie	Kaydee
Carl	Charley	Carlo
Elaine	Elena	Delaney
Dick	Rick	Brock

TORCH YOUR BOOKS

Here is one of the many ways that I can't—nay, won't!—stop acting old. I refuse to stop reading. I even insist on reading some things printed on actual paper (aka papyrus scrolls) and not containing four-color pictures.

People in my age and gender group—fiftyish women—are found in studies to be the most likely to read books, while our male counterparts are the only ones left reading newspapers. Young women are paging through celebrity mags and reading vampire romance graphic novels, while young males are playing *Grand Theft Auto*.

If you're not about to trade in *Anna Karenina* for Niko Bellic (if you don't know who that is, ask your teenage son), you may want to revisit your youth by reading Meg Cabot's *Forever Princess*, to remember when you thought love would solve everything; Erica Jong's *Fear of Flying*, to remember why you started having sex with everybody you could get your hands on; Sue Miller's *The Good Mother*, to remember why you stopped; and Sheila Weller's *Girls Like Us*, to remember the women you wished you were (and are ultimately glad you're not).

7 WAYS TO READ YOUNGER

OLD READING MATERIAL	YOUNG READING MATERIAL
Newspapers	Blogs
Historical romances	Vampire romances
Mysteries	Graphic novels
GQ	*Game Informer*
Stephen King	*Harry Potter*
The Grapes of Wrath	*Wicked*
O, The Oprah Magazine	*Cosmopolitan*

ENOUGH WITH THE SEINFELD, ALREADY!

Maybe you faithfully sat in front of the TV every Thursday night (remember those pre-TiVo days?) for *Seinfeld's* entire first run. Maybe you still catch the syndicated shows nearly every night, the same way that your parents watch *The Nightly News* and your kids watch *The Simpsons*. Maybe you've gotten the boxed sets as gifts over the past few years. And maybe you can genuinely relate nearly everything that happens in your life to a *Seinfeld* episode.

But listen, the real life Jerry has moved on. He's got a young wife, little kids, and a struggling new career as a voice actor; when you've got that much money, you can buy yourself a twenty-years-younger life. Larry David has moved on with his new family, *The Blacks*. All the other *Seinfeld* players have moved on to shows and futures of their own. OK, well, most of them.

12 OTHER CULTURAL REFERENCES SURE TO DATE YOU

1. *M.A.S.H.*
2. Watergate
3. *The Odd Couple*
4. Joey Buttafuoco
5. *Romper Room*
6. Either Kennedy assassination
7. *The Brady Bunch*
8. Paul Michael Glaser
9. Jean-Claude Killy
10. *Happy Days*
11. *Captain Kangaroo*
12. Woodstock

SAY YAY!

Happy? Excited? Managed to uncork the champagne, find a pair of Louboutins on sale in your size, land the job?

Here's what you say: yay! Not loudly and energetically, like you're a cheerleader at a football game. But softly and, well, coolly, with perhaps a little twist of your head. Yay! Be sure to infuse the word with a touch of irony but an equal measure of sincerity. You're happy. You know it. But you're way too cool to get embarrassingly carried away.

If the news is *really* amazing—let's say Ryan Reynolds leaves Blake Lively for you, or you win a reality show—you may accompany your yay with a little Snoopy-esque happy dance. A little one, I said: cute and never out of control.

Yelps, tears, "Oh, My God!"s, and other over-the-top expressions of joy are for the tacky and the old.

HOW NOT TO Vacation OLD

People say that one of the best things about getting older is that you finally have the time and freedom to travel. Except when you actually get older, it becomes a lot more difficult—psychologically, I mean, not canes and walkers difficult—to get yourself out of the house and on the road.

Here's how to transcend the traveling challenges that come with age:

BEFORE YOU GO:

Do Not Book Your Flights, Arrange Your Accommodations, or Plan Your Itinerary So Far Ahead that when the date gets near, you can no longer remember what airline you're flying on, what time you're leaving, or even exactly where you're going.

Resist the Temptation to Panic and Pack Your Entire Life. You don't need six pairs of shoes, clothing for every weather possibility from heat wave to gale-force blizzard, plus your special coffee and the pillow that keeps your spouse from snoring.

No Luggage Too Heavy for You to Actually Lift.

. . . and **No Luggage That Matches.** Unless it's Vuitton.

And **No Fanny Packs.** Even—make that especially—Vuitton.

If you ignore my advice about packing light, at least **Don't Bring Everything from Your Backup Sneakers to Three Purple Sweaters and Then Forget Your Life-Saving Medication.**

Don't Leave Your Plumber's Phone Number and Your Life Insurance Policy with Your Neighbor "just in case."

Speaking of "just in case," **You Don't Need to Wash the Last Sock in Your Eternal Laundry Pile and Pay All Your Bills before You Leave.** You are coming back—if you can ever actually get out of the house in the first place.

Don't Travel an Entire Three Miles from Home Only to Have to Turn around Because You Think You Might Have Left the Iron On. (Why do you have an iron?) Or because you think you might not have locked the door. Or because you have to go to the bathroom.

IF YOU'RE FLYING:

Do Not Get to the Airport Three and a Half Hours Ahead of Time. Yes, it takes a while to get through security these days: maybe seventeen minutes. Then you've still got a whole three hours and thirteen minutes to kill, and there are only so many Auntie Anne's pretzels a person can eat.

Do Not Dress Up for the Flight. Assuming you're neither the pilot nor a flight attendant, there is no need to wear a tie, skirt, hat with a shiny visor, shoes more formal than flip-flops, or a bra. If you feel sloppy, you can always add epaulets with gold stars to your pajamas.

Don't Make Friends with the person sitting next to you. Unless it's ScarJo.

IF YOU'RE DRIVING:

Don't Travel Five Miles off the Highway in Search of Gas That's Five Cents a Gallon Less. Modern math: the seventy-five cents you save won't even buy you a can of soda.

No Scenic Routes. Scenic routes, with their cows and their small towns, their speed traps and their no-passing zones, are old—and they're often not even that scenic anymore.

If you get lost and have to pull into a gas station to ask for directions, **Don't Keep Nodding As If You Totally Understand and Then Turn the Wrong Way** right out of the parking lot. Not that you've ever done that, honey.

ACCOMMODATIONS:

Do Not Stay at One of Those Inns That Smell Like Air Freshener and offer an assortment of herbal teas and have little signs posted everywhere that say things like "Thank you for removing your makeup before putting your head on the pillow!" You know, those signs that make you want to go out and buy some makeup just so you can rub foundation into the pillow.

If You Stay at a Chain Motel Instead of One of Those Inns, Don't Say, "You Have a Nice Room." They're all nice. They're all identical.

Don't Rent a House and Car Exactly Like the house and car you have at home.

ONCE YOU'RE THERE:

Don't Spend More Time Putting on Sunscreen than you spend in the sun.

Forget Shopping. You already brought too much stuff in your giant suitcase.

Don't Be the First One in the Restaurant at breakfast—not to mention dinner.

No Guided Tours. In fact, No Tourism. You're a traveler. No, you're practically a native! If you see a tourist or a tour, act appropriately scornful.

Don't Be Afraid to Go Somewhere Brand-New. They will definitely have bathrooms there—plus some kind of food that doesn't upset your stomach.

Don't Overworry about the Weather. Vacation like the young do. If the weather gets bad, you can... stay busy... in the hotel room.

If You're Traveling Alone and End Up Having Sex with a Stranger, Don't Imagine That You're Ever Going to See Him or Her Again. But don't feel guilty about it, either. If you're traveling with your spouse and end up having sex with a stranger, you should of course feel guilty. But way not to act old, dude or dudette! You and John Edwards should totally get together.

WHEN YOU'RE BACK HOME:

Don't Claim That Now You Need Another Vacation. That's not just old, it's obnoxious!

DON'T LIVE IN A BIG HOUSE AND COMPLAIN ABOUT MONEY

We get it that maybe you bought your house a couple of booms ago when prices were low, so you're really not as rich as you look. We understand that the taxes on a house that big are through the roof (so to speak), and you don't even want to think about what your heating bill is going to be this year.

And to all that we say: oh, boo hoo.

If you're lucky and old enough to live in a big house or a sprawling apartment you bought in 1986 for $200,000, you're not allowed to complain. Yes, even if you've got cash flow problems—even if you're only halfway through putting the second kid through college. If you need money so badly, sell the house and move into the kind of place you can buy for $200,000 these days: an RV.

6 WAYS TO RENOVATE YOUR MONEY COMPLAINTS

1. **Instead of:** "My property taxes just went up again."
   Say: "I could have saved the tax on that pair of Louboutins by having them shipped to my parents' house in Jersey, but the humiliation wasn't worth it."

2. **Instead of:** "I had to work all last night balancing my checkbook."
   Say: "I don't think I ever got a checkbook."

3. **Instead of:** "My kids' tuition is going up again."
   Say: "My parents don't have a right to see my grades just because they pay my tuition."

4. **Instead of:** "Can you believe how much a Chanel bag costs these days?"
   Say: "A Chanel bag is worth it because it makes everyone take you seriously."

5. **Instead of:** "Can you believe how much A-Rod made last year?"
   Say: "If I only had a thousand dollars, I could stop worrying about money."

6. **Instead of:** "I had to pay $3.79 for mustard."
   Say: "Isn't mustard, like, free?"

SCRATCH THAT GOLF GAME

Some sports are young, and some sports are old. Examples?

Basketball is young; baseball is old.

Snowboarding is young; skiing is old.

Skateboarding is young; roller-skating is old.

And golf is old. So old I can't even think of something similar-yet-different (miniature golf? No. Croquet? Nah.) to put on the young side of the equation.

Why? It's expensive, for one thing. It's slow; not all that strenuous; the outfits are not very cute. And the shoes!

Plus, golf takes planning—you need to reserve the course days, weeks, or even years in advance. And it takes patience, a quality that tends to increase with age.

The only thing about golf that has any youth appeal are the carts. I would like to ride around a golf course in one of those carts. I just don't want to have to wear shoes with cleats or knock any little balls out of the sand.

86

TURN YOUR STEREO UP AND YOUR TV DOWN

Why do our senses get selectively better or worse as we get older? Suddenly we can't hear the television at all, and have to keep pumping up the volume until we all but blast younger folk out of the room. Yet at the same time, music any louder than a lullaby is painful to our ears.

It's been forty years since I took any kind of science class—and I think I got a D in that one—but empirically this evidence would seem to suggest that the problem is not really in our hearing *per se*, but in our sensibilities. So one solution might be to pay closer attention to what the people are saying on television, and at the same time turn up the music the way you did when you were twenty-two.

Of course, it's also possible that all the loud music we listened to in our youth has actually made us deaf, and that at the same time we've become crankier.

UNLESS YOU'RE IN NAGASAKI, DON'T GIVE (OR ASK FOR) DIRECTIONS

O nce, looking for a swimming hole in Maine, a local told me to turn left where the old school burned down. That's what giving directions is like these days. In this era of Mapquest and GPS, it's meaningless to tell someone to turn left at the church, go under the railroad trestle, and look for the yellow house.

Let the computer do the work for you. If the other person gets lost, blame it on their digital guide. When we all have chips implanted in our brains, we'll never again have any need to know where we are or where we're going; we'll just go wherever Google tells us.

NO HOVERING

Dear Marge,

I realize that, in the 396 public bathrooms I've visited in the past week on the road, someone else might have been the culprit. But the fact is, the only one I really suspect is you.

I know your mom told you that sitting on the seat of a public toilet could give you a disease. Mommy watched to make sure you hovered over the toilet without letting anything touch anything else. Ever since, you've found it impossible to allow yourself to actually sit down on a public toilet, so instead you pee half-standing up.

But your aging thighs aren't up to holding you steady, so guess what, Marge: you sprinkle the seat. You flush and leave, and when I enter the stall, there is your pee left all over for ME to sit in. Or clean up. Maybe you feel all clean and smug and satisfied because YOU avoided sitting on the public toilet seat. But did you ever stop to think about what you're doing to me?

DON'T COOK THE ROAST

It's an unwritten law of the universe: no one under the age of forty knows how to cook a roast. No one under the age of forty *wants* to know how to cook a roast. A roast symbolizes childhood Sundays, dinner with the relatives, and leftovers. Besides, cooking the roast is *Mom's* job, not ours.

And then, at some point in middle age, most of us realize that a roast is not only delicious and substantial but just about the easiest thing to cook. Eight for dinner? Twelve for Christmas? Sixty for an open house? All you need is a meat thermometer and a giant hunk of beef, pork, or lamb, and dinner's done.

It's guaranteed that your younger friends and relatives will be grateful, not to mention awed, that you cooked that magnificent roast. But they won't respect you for it. Instead, they'll assign you a permanent apron, a gray bun, and a pair of rimless spectacles plastered to the tip of your oven-scorched nose.

12 STEPS TO MAKING DINNER YOUNG

1. **Pour yourself** a large glass of wine. Swearing that you waste time and money going out to dinner or ordering takeout every night, make up your mind to cook.
2. Select a **lively playlist** to keep you company.
3. Open a **bag of chips.** It's not smart to cook on an empty stomach. Or is that shop?
4. **Go to a recipe site**—recipematcher.com is one—that helps you figure out what you can cook based on what's in your refrigerator. Let's see: gnocchi from the restaurant the other night, a half carton of olives, and some moldy strawberries. We got nothin'.
5. In order to do a **proper grocery shop,** you'd have to buy a car and move to the suburbs, a considerably more expensive enterprise than ordering takeout. Pour yourself another glass of wine.
6. **Wish you were** one of those worldly people who could conjure dinner from thin air. A little oil, a little garlic, a little pasta . . .
7. Hey, you have **oil, garlic, and pasta!** Heat oil, peel garlic, boil water for pasta, feeling pretty damn worldly after all.
8. **Multitask** by checking iPhone while water boils. You're so domestic, you're so adept; you might be ready to have a baby after all!
9. Ooops, **work emergency!** By the time you clear it, garlic has fried to nothing and pot has boiled itself black.
10. **Significant other arrives** home to find you in tears. A few kisses and hugs later, feel not only comforted but distinctly amorous. Forgetting hunger, make love.
11. A few hours later, **stomachs growling,** revisit the dinner situation. Options: Manny's Indian Takeout (again) or Maria's Corner Trattoria (again). But you swore you were going to make dinner yourself!
12. **Solution:** one jar of peanut butter. Two spoons.

DON'T LUST AFTER THE LIFEGUARD

When you were thirteen, you had the hugest crush on the lifeguard who totally ignored you. Then, when you were nineteen or twenty-three, the lifeguard may have lusted after you—but you decided he was too shallow to warrant your attention. When you were thirty-five, you were too busy making sure the kids didn't drown to notice him.

It's only now that you're able to fully appreciate the lifeguard's virtues, and to fantasize that maybe he appreciates yours in return. This is the point at which you have to imagine me slapping you across the face and crying, "Snap out of it!"

Unless we're talking about the world's Oldest Living Lifeguard—you know, the one whose skin is so weathered you could make a purse out of it—the lifeguard is too young for you.

10 SIGNS YOU MIGHT BE A LECH

1. You think the babysitter is hot for you.
2. Your favorite romantic screen couple is Woody Allen and Mariel Hemingway in *Manhattan*.
3. When your assistant compliments your shoes, you think she means it.
4. You skip the game, but watch the halftime show.
5. You really think the Monica Lewinsky thing was unfair to Bill.
6. That time you drove a convertible, you thought everyone was looking at you—I mean, looking at you favorably.
7. You have your own subscription to *Glamour*.
8. You comb over.
9. You flirt with the counter girl at McDonald's.
10. You think your son's girlfriend likes him because he looks like you.

DEHYPHENATE YOUR NAME

There was a brief moment when name hyphenization seemed like the answer to all marital equality issues. A moment when two people might have gotten married and become Pamela and Richard Redmond-Satran. (Not that we did that: my husband declined to take the Redmond, so I just dragged both names behind me like a big fat butt, without even a hyphen to connect them.)

But back to you: the whole hyphen thing seemed like a good idea for about a minute and a half, until the jokes started about what would happen when Gabriella Redmond-Satran (not one of our real children) married Marmaduke Martini-O'Flaherty. Would their child be called Maximilian Redmond-Satran-Martini-O'Flaherty?

And then there was the question of whose name went first, and whether the husband as well as the wife would adopt the hyphen, until the notion just collapsed. Before that happened, however, several hundred people got married and hyphenated their names. All those people are now over the age of fifty—or just sound like it.

QUIT BOSSING EVERYBODY AROUND

So you think you know it all, do you? Think you're so on top of everything that you know what everybody else should be doing—and don't hesitate to tell them?

I've seen this phenomenon before, on the first few seasons of *Survivor*. It was always the older competitors who thought they had such superior experience in hut-building, berry-picking, and fish-spearing that they could organize the whole camp and tell everyone what to do, and that that would make their teammates respect and value them.

And guess what happened? That's right: they were voted off. The young hotties would sit there and smile and nod and then go to tribal council and *zap*. So you be a smiler and a nodder, too, and the boss of only yourself.

NO MATCHING ANYTHING

Matching marks you as belonging to an earlier time and sensibility, when all things had to be tidily coordinated and anyone who was sane and solvent bought everything from their jewelry to their living room furniture to their luggage to their bathroom accessories—down to the toilet paper roll covers—in complete sets.

This is an aesthetic that went out with matching Villager sweaters and kneesocks. Yet—perhaps influenced by catalog retailers, who have an interest in making you feel as if you need to buy the chair and the end table and the rug and the pillows that go with the sofa as pictured—overmatching lives on. But matched anything belies a certain insecurity, a lack of imagination, that can make you seem stodgy and old-fashioned and just plain old.

So go ahead, unmatch. Wear silver with gold, brown with black, suede with patent. Put Grandma's Victorian armchair next to your Crate & Barrel midcentury couch; sling a Vera Bradley duffle over your shoulder and roll a stainless-steel spinner. The less you match, the freer you'll feel—and the younger you'll seem.

5 WAYS NOT TO HOLIDAY OLD

Some holidays are getting younger, while others are getting older—July 4, younger, but Memorial Day and Labor Day, older. Halloween is getting way younger and cooler, while Easter is crumbling into decrepitude.

Christmas is evergreen, but New Year's Eve and Valentine's Day feel like holidays of the young, while Veteran's Day—though worthy—is ancient.

MLK Day: young. Presidents' Day: old.

Here, some holiday behavior guidelines.

1. **No Lame Holiday Nicknames.** Forget "Our Nation's Birthday," "Turkey Day," "St. Paddy's Day": not only old, but lame.

2. **Don't Hang One of Those Flag Bunting Things on Your Front Porch.** Very DAR: colonial, dowdy, old. Though I have to admit I have a perverse fondness for these half-circle flags and have one I bought at a yard sale years ago that I can neither bring myself to hang nor get rid of.

3. **Don't Plant Your Metal Folding Chair Right at the Curb on the Parade Route.** Let the little kids hog the front rows. You stand gracefully in back, and if you get tired, go home and take a nice nap.

4. **No Overthemed Food.** No red, white, and blue potato salad, no cupcakes with little hearts sticking out of them, no turkey-shaped Jell-O mold. Although Jell-O molds might be so old they're young again.

5. **Watch Those Oooohs and Aaaahs.** There seems to be an inverse relationship between the number of times someone has seen fireworks and their audible expressions of approval, with grannies, who ought to be so jaded they barely glance skyward, invariably the most vocal. I was going to say you should therefore contain yourself, but you know what, screw it. If getting old means you're more comfortable showing your excitement over an everyday wonder, bring on the birthdays. *Oooooh!*

DON'T COUNT OUT *Exact* CHANGE

You've been there: in line behind the middle-aged woman who says, "Wait a minute! I think I have the exact change!" and then proceeds to rummage through the recesses of her bag in search for the precise assortment of quarters, dimes, nickels, and pennies that make up the price of her knee-high hose or chicken pot pie.

The reasoning seems to be that, if you pay for something with exact change, you at one stroke declutter your purse and get whatever you're buying for less. You've traded in all those heavy, jangly spare coins for a nourishing meat pie—and acted as if you're doing the poor cashier a big fat favor in the process.

But listen, change is inevitable. No matter how many pennies you get rid of, more will always come your way. And you're just annoying everybody in the meantime.

9 WAYS TO ANNOY OLD

1. Calculate the exact 15 percent tip (you haven't heard or don't care that it's 20 percent now).
2. Calculate the exact split of the bill.
3. Talk about the weather to strangers.
4. Ask the waiter or the clerk which entrée or pair of shoes you should get.
5. Call at 8:30 on Sunday morning, and act surprised that the other person is still asleep.
6. Send back your meal.
7. Be unable to find your wallet in your big old purse or bulging jacket.
8. Excitedly get everybody to listen to you, and then forget what you were going to say.
9. Sit in your car forever before pulling out of a parking space.

14 WAYS NOT TO ACT OLD AT A WEDDING

When you're young, you go to lots of weddings as all your friends get married. And then there's usually a dry spell for a couple of decades until your friends start getting remarried and your friends' and siblings' and cousins' kids get hitched. Entering the second round of weddings, you may find you're a little out of practice. Plus, some of the rules of decorum and seemliness may have changed along with your age and status. Here, how not to be one of those mortifying old people.

1. **Don't Buy a New Outfit.** You're not the bride. You're not a bridesmaid. You're not, God forbid, the mother (or father) of the bride, and you shouldn't dress like one. Just wear that nice outfit you wore to the last wedding you went to, even if it was eight years ago.

2. **Don't Wear Black.** Somewhere in the eighties, when black reigned supreme, it was declared that it was now okay to wear black to weddings. But today, wearing black to a wedding, especially if you're of a certain age, just seems a trifle world-weary, which never sits well when you actually are. Conversely, though, do not wear a Nile green floral skirt suit that may cause the wedding party to suffer epileptic seizures.

3. **Don't Start Sobbing Midway through the Ceremony** whether from sentimental joy or true sorrow for anyone foolish enough to get married. Pull up your socks and keep it yourself.

4. **When They Ask Whether Anyone Has Just Cause to Stop the Wedding,** keep quiet. See above.

5. **Do Not Attempt to Flirt with a Bridesmaid or Groomsman.** Leave those kinds of antics to the young people.

6. **Do Not Get Sloppy Drunk.** Yes, I'm speaking to you, dear.

7. **Don't Take the Cake Too Seriously.** Only old people go to weddings for the food.

8. **Don't Get Too Enthusiastic about the Macarena.** At every wedding, there's always one middle-aged woman who it's all too clear doesn't get out to dance nearly enough. Every rendition of the Macarena, of "Saturday Night Fever," of "Let's Boogie Tonight" has her on her feet and in the middle of the floor, partner or not, even if everybody else is in the other room watching the cake get cut. Usually, that woman is me. But I swear I'm going to stop.

9. **Stop That Glass-Clinking Stuff.** It might be argued that bullying the bride and groom into kissing is not only lecherous but politically incorrect.

10. **Don't Skimp on Your Gift.** Calculate the value of your gift based on the per-head cost of the wedding, which would probably be at least $100 these days.

11. **But You Don't Have to Go Crazy.** Some modern weddings are so over-the-top—destination events that include several days of festivities—that buying a gift truly commensurate with the cost of your being there would be outrageous, especially when you consider the cost of getting to and being at the wedding. Be generous, but not as if you're trying to stay in the good graces of Don Corleone.

12. **No Mama Drama.** Your niece's wedding is not the time to confront your sister-in-law about not bringing the right kind of pie to last Thanksgiving's dinner.

13. **Don't Grab the Bouquet.** Let somebody truly optimistic catch it.

14. **As Tracey Ullman Says, Go Home.** Leave the young people to dance the last dance and shut down the bar. Isn't it your bedtime?

STOP ALL THAT MOVING AROUND

Here's a counterintuitive directive: if you want not to act old, you've got to knock off all that surfing, skating, basketball playing, and cardio-kickboxing you've evidently been doing. Lying on the couch, staying out of the gym, and sitting on the sidelines are the sports of the young, while middle-aged and older people are the ones who are joining ice hockey teams and wearing themselves out on elliptical trainers.

So says a new British study, which found that more and more middle-aged and older people are exercising and playing sports, while fewer young people are exercising now than were ten years ago. My scientific analysis: we've been doing all that kayaking and cycling in a misguided attempt to be thinner and more limber—aka younger—and to stave off dying. The evil young, meanwhile, say "Ha! We're thin and limber without even trying. And we know we're never gonna die."

Well, "Ha!" back atcha, evil young. I now know there's an infinitely easier and more effective way to act younger: sit on my big fat ass. So *sayonara*, Zumba. Bye-bye, Bikram. If I lounge here long enough, everybody's going to think I'm twenty-eight again.

DON'T BE A CHICKEN

Old people certainly don't have a monopoly on fear. Some fears—spiders, public speaking, even flying—may even be ones we've faced and conquered. But change and novelty, not so much. The fear of newness even has a name: caicophobia.

Maybe you're afraid to try a different haircut, since your current style has worked so well for you since 1993. Vacation in Virginia instead of Vermont? Undergo hypnosis, or attempt bungee jumping? Chicken, chicken, chicken, chicken. Not to mention the scariness inherent in doing something like moving across the country or changing careers, which forces you back into the position of being a rank beginner and therefore relatively ignorant and powerless, not a comfortable position for those of us who've achieved some measure of security and stature in our lives.

But being afraid to embrace the unknown can shorten your lifespan, at least if you're a rat. One study shows that scaredy-cat rats die sooner than adventuresome ones. You're safer bungee jumping than you are stressing over what will happen if you take the leap.

8 FEAR-CONQUERING IDEAS

IF YOU'RE AFRAID OF . . .	TRY . . .
Going back to school	Teaching a class
Moving to a city apartment	Renting an apartment for vacation
Going into the weight room	Hiring a trainer
Building a Web site	Starting a blog
Setting up Roku	Joining Netflix
Going on vacation alone	Going on a singles tour
Wearing a bathing suit at the beach	Swimming for exercise

HOLD THE MOO GOO GAI PANT

When we first tasted "ethnic" food, what counted as exotic and exciting was some stew made of indefinable ingredients and bearing a funny name: moo goo gai pan, spaghetti puttanesca, pad Thai, the pu pu platter.

But in this era of McDonald's sushi (trust me; it's coming) and Indian frozen dinners, it's time to update your palate. Try the cold jelly Chengdu style. The kaiseki ryori. As long as you move beyond ordering the same thing you've been getting since you were nineteen, you'll be fine.

OLD FOOD/YOUNG FOOD: 18 CULINARY COMPARISONS

OLD FOOD	YOUNG FOOD
Shrimp cocktail	Kumamoto oysters
Filet mignon	Hanger steak
Pork chop	Pork belly
Sauerbrauten	Kavalierspitz
Tuna tartare	Tuna cheek sashimi
Grilled swordfish	Arctic char, poached *sous vide*
Brunswick stew	Texas-style BBQ
Chicken teriyaki	Chicken lollipops
Spaghetti with clam sauce	Sea urchin risotto
Eggplant parmigiana	Roasted ramps
Chardonnay	Muscadet
Fried eggs	Deep-fried poached egg
Tuna melt	Banh mi
White bread	Pain au levain
Flan	Kulfi
Eclairs	Mochi
Ice cream	Pinkberry
Irish coffee	Dark & Stormy

STEP AWAY
FROM THE
GIANT
PUMPKIN

One of the fascinating and bizarre things I've noticed recently is that middle-aged men love to grow giant pumpkins. Not a few guys in some isolated pumpkin patch, mind you, but a whole "giant pumpkin community" that spans the globe, organizes scores of competitions every fall, and even hosts an annual convention.

Is it coincidence that most giant pumpkin enthusiasts are men in their fifties? I think not. People in their fifties seem to take up all sorts of weird hobbies and enthusiasms, from cultivating hydrangeas to investigating the family tree to collecting painted tin dachshunds to developing a gourmet cuisine based entirely on seaweed.

I guess this is what happens when the kids are grown, the mortgage is paid off, and you've decided not to get a dog or a divorce. Everything else has been scratched off your life list, and what's left? "Instead of having an affair, leaving you, or getting hair plugs, I'm just going to grow a pumpkin as big as a flippin' house, honey. Don't wait up."

FALL IS SO NOT YOUR FAVORITE SEASON

Favorite season of the old: fall. Why? Because the colors are so lovely, you get to wear clothes that cover your body again, and you're forced to stay in the house and eat beef stew and apple pie and drink sidecars.

Sounds pretty good to me, but not to the young. For young people, fall means a return to school (blech) even years after they've graduated. No more bikinis, no more beach, goodbye to the summer share. Second and third place go to spring, as in fever, and winter, for the snowboarding and the nice Christmas check from mom and dad.

8 OTHER FAVORITES YOU MAY WANT TO RETHINK

1. Favorite Color: Grayish-green.
2. Favorite Holiday: Thanksgiving.
3. Favorite Day of the Week: Thursday. Or maybe Sunday.
4. Favorite Music: Classical. Or maybe jazz.
5. Favorite Vegetable: Brussels sprouts.
6. Favorite City: London.
7. Favorite Skirt Style: Pleated.
8. Favorite Weather: Cool and rainy.

SAY THAYNK KYEEEW

Here's a weird little sociological etymological glitch: young women say "thank you" differently than you or I. Perhaps they feel more entitled, thus the simper that colors the phrase when it comes from their lips. Or maybe those words have become so automatic that they feel obligated to add a layer of irony.

Whatever the cause, what the young say sounds more like "thaynk," with a really heeeey-like "a," and then "you" with a really long eeew-like sound. The "thank" is said quickly, with a kind of clanky clippedness, while the "you" is drawn out. The "k" is pronounced at both the end of thank and the beginning of you. The result: "thaynk kyeeew."

GARAGE
YOUR
HOG

aving just returned from a 700-mile road trip, I can tell you with certainty that every motorcyclist on the American highway is at least fifty-six years old. All the biker babes have Nice 'n Easy covering their gray and pot bellies straining against their leather pants. Motorcyclists may think that roaring along on a hog makes them look cool, or young, but as an elderly vehicle of choice, bikes are right up there with Winnebagos.

How did motorcyles go from being a symbol of youthful rebellion to one of middle-aged desperation? The timeline begins with Marlon Brando looking young and hot in *The Wild One* in 1953. Hippies and bikers united in their countercultural beliefs in the 1960s—until Altamont. A fan was killed, a riot ensued, and the image of motorcyclists went from cool to terrifying in two seconds flat.

It got even weirder after that, when a band of Hells Angels plotted to kill Mick Jagger, attacking the Hamptons by boat.

These image problems discouraged young people from taking up motorcycling over the past few decades, so now most of the active motorcyclists are middle-aged or older. If it's youthfulness you're after, trade in that hog for something more daring, like racing junk. Or a fixed-gear bicycle: look Ma, no brakes!

14 THINGS THAT USED TO BE YOUNG BUT ARE NOW OLD

1. Leather jackets
2. Folk music
3. VW Bugs
4. Modern dance
5. Sausalito
6. Cigarettes
7. Group therapy sessions
8. Hamburgers
9. Astrology
10. The Grateful Dead
11. Berets
12. Black turtlenecks

13. Wine
14. Candy

17 THINGS THAT USED TO BE OLD BUT ARE NOW YOUNG

1. Hair dye
2. Bow ties
3. Bob Dylan
4. Manhattans
5. Politics
6. Hermès scarves
7. Fords
8. Pigs in blankets
9. Poetry
10. Las Vegas
11. Tea
12. Cigars
13. Big formal weddings
14. Big glasses
15. Poker
16. Hats
17. Rubber galoshes

STIFLE
THE ANDY ROONEY
RANTS

You may think that there's no chance you're anything like Andy Rooney. You would never, after all, rant about why pencils are just as good as computers or try to make a case for the revival of the apron.

But you may inadvertently be channeling Andy if you carry on about any of the following:

The ridiculousness of contemporary baby names, epitomized by the child—you swear, your sister-in-law the nurse saw it with her own eyes—who was named Gonorrhea.

The failure of young people today to move out of their parents' houses, get married, and assume adult responsibilities before the age of, say, forty-three.

The inflated cost of handbags.

NO BRAS THE SIZE OF WYOMING

As the years advance, we full-figured gals have a, ahem, weighty challenge ahead of us. How do we hoist the girls as high as possible without resorting to a bra the size of Wyoming?

The answer, as with so many things, is money. Any bra that's going to do its considerable job and still look feminine, attractive, and young is going to set you back at least as much as you just spent on sneakers for your teenager. You're going to have to go to a fancy lingerie department to buy it, and even be fitted by a trained professional brandishing a tape measure.

Let's just quickly run over the elements your bra *cannot* have: no elastic thick and strong enough to support a bungee jumper; no more than two—or, in extreme cases, three—hooks in back; no cups so capacious they totally rule out the possibility of cleavage; no quadriboob; no backfat.

At the same time, your bra needs to lift, separate, streamline, steady, and smooth. Impossible? No. Expensive but worth it? Absolutely.

DON'T FEAR THE BIRTHDAY

Of course it sucks to see those numbers mount up. But don't deny the birthday. Look at it this way: nobody has to know how old you are to justify a celebration. By this point in life we all know we have to seize pleasure and attention whenever and however we can get it—which is never often enough.

So don't shy away from the dinner, the party, the presents, the cake, and yes, even a big blazing forest of candles to mark another successful year of holding your head up high.

MADLIBS: HOW TO CELEBRATE YOUR BIRTHDAY RIGHT

To have a really great birthday party, invite __number__ of your closest friends to __place__. Serve __kind of drink__ and __kind of food__ , and decorate the place with lots of __plural noun__ and __plural noun__ . A theme, such as __animals__ or __color__ , can help make the event more __adjective__ .

Be sure to play __game__ and sing __name of song__ . Everyone has to __verb__ the birthday boy or girl. Don't forget to open the gifts; people will enjoy watching your reaction to such items as __plural noun__ and __plural noun__ . And for the final touch, try to blow out all __number__ ~ __plural noun__ on your __adjective__ cake.

DON'T GO *Hatin' on* CHRISTMAS

Hating Christmas is an affliction peculiar to the old. Why? Let me count the ways.

- It's expensive, and we have to pay for it.
- It's a lot of work, and we have to do all of it.
- We are really, really, *really* sure there's no Santa.
- There was that time we got drunk and had a huge fight with our spouse on Christmas Eve. Also, that other time. And the time when our mother-in-law started screaming at us about not getting her a nice enough present. And the time we threw up in the mashed potatoes. And the time . . . oh, never mind. The point is once you've been around for enough Christmases, you accumulate plenty of bad memories along with the good.
- It's cold, and we no longer like the cold.
- It's almost never a white Christmas, and if it is, we have to shovel it.
- We're exhausted.
- We have too much work to do as it is.
- Nobody ever wants to kiss us under the mistletoe.

We could go on, but we're getting kinda bummed out already. Let's just say we have our reasons for hating Christmas, and they're good ones, but at the same time we're making ourselves seem, not to mention feel, older by being such Grinches.

How to renovate your Xmas outlook?

Well, you could slip a diamond into your own Christmas stocking. Surprise everyone on Christmas Eve with tickets to Barbados and nothing for Christmas dinner in the refrigerator. Give all your money to a worthy charity and so create inner peace and an ironclad excuse for skipping the whole damn thing in one stroke of genius.

Or just develop an appreciation for single-malt scotch and chocolate-chip meringues, and pass the season in an alcohol-and-sugar haze. Here's the recipe:

CHOCOLATE-CHIP MERINGUE COOKIES

Ingredients

2 large egg whites
1/8 teaspoon cream of tartar
1/2 cup granulated sugar
1 tablespoon cocoa powder (optional)
1 teaspoon vanilla extract
1 1/2 cups semisweet chocolate chips or chocolate chunks (or even M&Ms)

Directions

Preheat oven to 275°F. Line 2 cookie sheets with parchment paper.

With electric mixer on high, whip egg whites until foamy. Add cream of tartar and whip until soft peaks form. Add sugar slowly, whipping until stiff but not dry peaks form. (The whole "stiff peaks" thing sometimes fails me here, but never mind. Whip 'til it seems like they're as stiff as they're ever going to be, then give up and carry on.)

Beat in cocoa powder and vanilla. Fold in chocolate chips. Bake until completely firm and dry, but still white, about 35–45 minutes; you should be able to lift cookies from pan. You can turn off the oven but leave meringues inside for an hour if you like crunchier meringues.

DON'T TRY TO BE AS THIN AS TWIGGY

At thirteen, I aspired to have a figure like Twiggy's—and I wasn't far off, either. Twiggy and I were both built like, well, twigs, and keeping that thin was disgustingly effortless.

Well, things have changed, and even Twiggy isn't immune from middle-aged spread; she limits her diet to one chocolate square at a time, she says, and "one pudding a month" or risks bloating up like every other over-forty.

There goes the myth of the naturally thin person who stays that way forever. If even Twiggy porks up, what hope is there for the rest of us?

Extra nondiet tip: don't reference Twiggy in relation to thinness, weight loss, or modeling. Young people won't have any idea who you're talking about. Kate Moss, maybe. Doutzen or Agyness (born Laura) Deyn: now you're talking.

12 OTHER PEOPLE AND THINGS THAT WON'T DISAPPEAR ANY-TIME SOON (NO MATTER HOW MUCH YOU WISH THEY WOULD)

1. Jeans as tight as leggings
2. Leggings instead of pants
3. Nose studs
4. Miniskirts
5. Hip-hop music
6. Reality TV
7. High-heeled ankle boots
8. Tops that make you look pregnant
9. *Family Guy*
10. Bikinis
11. iPods
12. Emoticons :(

DON'T PUT IT IN CRUISE CONTROL

Remember cruise control? When I was a kid, I couldn't wait to grow up and get myself a fancy car with cruise control. I'd set that baby to seventy-five miles per hour, sit back, and feel like one of the Jetsons.

Well, I now have a car with cruise control. I guess. The fact is that I've never used it. My husband has never used it. I even forgot what it was called until I went out and looked in the manual just now. The last person I heard of using cruise control was my father-in-law, back in the nineties, and it seemed like a relic even then.

Cruise control is one of those technological innovations that was futuristic until it was suddenly *passé*. The subject of acting old as it connects to cars and driving can be confusing. Is it older to drive a hot red sports car or a big old Cadillac? To creep along hunched over the wheel or drive like a maniac?

But when it comes to putting it in cruise control, literally as well as figuratively, the connection is clear. Which reminds me of a joke told today in the writing class I'm taking with the divine Lynda Barry, author of the excellent new book *What It Is*, who is either the youngest old person I've ever met or the world's oldest living child. Here's Lynda's joke:

One day Hank and Mo, two old-in-every-sense-of-the-word friends, went out for a drive. They came to a stop sign, and Hank sailed right through. Mo was nervous but didn't say anything. They came to another stop sign, and again, Hank didn't even slow down. Then they came to a red light, and Hank just kept going, barely avoiding oncoming cars.

Finally, Mo had to speak up. "Hank," he said, "why didn't you stop at those stop signs and that red light?"

"Oh," Hank said. "Am I driving?"

DON'T TALK TO STRANGERS

Maybe what happened is that everybody up to the age of, oh, thirty had the "Don't talk to strangers" directive drilled so hard into their heads that it's second nature for them to keep to themselves. In airports, in kickboxing class, in line at the bank, they tend to keep their eyes trained on their phones or the mirror and not to make eye contact or strike up animated casual conversations.

Not the way that we do—or at least that I do. I'll talk to anybody, anywhere. In fact, I'm often looking for the chance to swap comments on train schedules or coffee orders or whether that skirt we're both trying on is flattering. Finding myself alone on an airplane or in a restaurant, I'm likely to walk out with a new friend.

However, that new friend is unlikely to be under forty. And if I start talking to strangers in the vicinity of my children, they react as if I spontaneously started dancing and singing "Let's Get It On" right there in the street.

So if you want not to act old, stop making those random comments in yoga class or asking the woman in the waiting room whether she likes the book she's reading. But if you want to stay happy, just keep doing it when no one young is watching.

NO
ARCADE FIRE
OR PORKPIE HATS

It's one thing for an ancient (that's you, baby) to keep abreast (there's an old word) of popular culture and stay aware of what the young and hipsterish are doing just to torture you.

But it's quite another to attempt to actually be a hipster. You may think you can deconstruct all the elements of hipsterhood—the Yoo-hoo T-shirts and the Regina Spektor records (yeah, they're back), the vegan diet and the loft in Williamsburg and the toddler named Leta—and then you will be a hipster. But you're forgetting the most important thing it takes to be a hipster; you have to be young.

How young? If you have to ask: younger than you. So give it up, dollface. Put the aviator shades in the case, find a long-sleeved shirt to cover up the crown o' thorns inked on your bicep, and stop calling everything fierce.

You're sure to win as much admiration for all your acquired wisdom as you did for your mint green Vespa, right? As if.

8 ITEMS OF HIPSTER GEAR YOU CAN GET AWAY WITH

1. Granddad cardigan
2. Orthopedic sandals from Germany
3. Skinny tie
4. Ray-Ban frames with prescription lenses
5. Heavy beard
6. Ranch house in Portland, Oregon
7. Stocking cap
8. Dress worn over jeans

8 ITEMS OF HIPSTER GEAR YOU CAN'T

1. Cosby sweater
2. Motorcycle boots from Germany
3. Keffiyeh scarf
4. Ray-Ban frames with clear lenses
5. Mussed-up hair
6. Loft in Bed-Stuy
7. Flip-rim hat
8. Shorts worn over stockings

DON'T WALK SMALL

Here's, ahem, one step to looking and feeling younger instantly: take big steps. That's right—biiiiiiig, wide, bold steps. Go ahead, try it. It really is like magic.

And once you start walking bigger, you'll be amazed to realize that you've been shuffling around with those little timid I-have-to-be-careful-or-I-could-topple-over-and-break-a-hip steps. You'll see that, with most people, steps get smaller and smaller with each passing year, with teenagers walking like the Keep on Truckin' guy and your grandma mincing along like a ballerina *en pointe*.

Keep on truckin', baby.

ACKNOWLEDGEMENTS

An old person could never develop a Web site and write a book called *How Not to Act Old* without considerable help.

My first thanks go to my smart, funny, graphically astute, and insightful research assistant Danielle Miksza, who was my main spy in the house of the young and aid in turning the blog into this book. Danielle told me what young people drank on Saturday night and how old people acted on Monday morning, among many other inside details that found their way into this text.

My children, Rory, Joe, and Owen Satran, also provided essential help and research. When I first started the blog, Joe would come home from his summer job at the *Huffington Post* to tell me how to code my pictures so they'd float inside the text. A knowledgeable foodie, he helped parse the list of old food and young food in the book. Owen provided my very first blog entry—who over twenty ever heard, never mind said, the words "Yo, you copped fire, son"?—and also detailed the difference between a brotha and a bro. And my daughter Rory, though she still won't be my friend on Facebook, did help me figure out how not to Facebook old and also came up with my hilarious subtitle.

I'm lucky enough to have an awesome—and I don't say that lightly—agent, Deborah Schneider, who not only loved the blog from the start but found me a fabulous book detail mere weeks after I launched. Thank you, Deborah.

If I were to design my ideal publisher—just one of my megalomaniacal fantasies—it would surely be *Harper Collins*, with its books that manage to combine beauty and brains and fun and edginess: hey, much like myself! Thank you in particular to my initial editor Nancy Miller, long lost friend and colleague of my youth, and to Jennifer Schulkind, who brought fresh enthusiasm and ideas to the project. I'd also like to thank assistant editor Molly Lindley and publishers Mary Ellen O'Neill and Carrie Kania.

My friends, colleagues, and readers of the blog helped me believe I should keep exploring the subject and contributed their own experiences for my amusement and the edification of all. Also, a couple hundred of my loved ones contributed wonderful title ideas, though I ended up doing, as usual, what I wanted to do from the beginning.

I'd like to especially thank the fabulous photographer Alexa Garbarino, who helped me figure out what this book might look like; Christina Baker Kline, who loved it from the beginning; Dorothea Benton Frank, who sent it to so many people it found its way to Meg Cabot; Meg Cabot, who blogged about it, sending thousands of her fans my way, and then blurbed it; Laurie Lico Albanese, always ready with good sense and inspiration; Alice Elliott Dark, who told me about walking large and FUPAs; Hugh Hunter, who told me that I and all my aged friends had to learn to dial and type with our thumbs; Diana Biederman, for the "21" Club splendor; Rita DiMatteo, who told me planning was old (undoubtedly while we were planning something together); Judy Coyne, for inspiring me to write like this in the first place and who, with the lovely Lesley Jane Seymour, adapted it for *More* magazine; and my husband Dick Satran, who kept reminding me to make it funny, not depressing.

Fellow bloggers and friends who helped spread the word include the inspirational Debbie Galant of Baristanet; Holly Cara Price of snoopdujour.com; Jen Singer, who writes for *Good Housekeeping*; Mauigirl52; and Rob Robinson of thinktrain.net, who called me "Stuff Old People Like," which still tickles. Anya Streitman and Verena Von Pfetten of the *Huffington Post* gave me a platform outside my own venue. My writing partners Linda Rosenkrantz and Kimberly Bonnell always delight and illuminate and support, whether we're working together or not.

Obviously, a book that starts out as a blog includes a lot more ideas and opinions than your usual nearly solo effort. Others I'd like to acknowledge include Henry Seltzer, Deborah and Dana Jennings, Cathy Gleason, Sheila Weller, Elliot Pinsley and Leslie Brody, Dave and Christina Baker Kline, Alexis Romay, Eric Levin, Toni Martin, Amy Edelman, and to the extraordinary photographer Fran Liscio for suggesting an LOL title that I hope someday will find its rightful book: *I Scored Some Eileen Fisher Caftans and That Shit Was Bangin'.*

ABOUT THE AUTHOR

PAMELA REDMOND SATRAN is the *New York Times* bestselling author of *Younger*, a new *TV Land* series by Darren Star, along with five other novels. She is also the author of three humor books, including *How Not To Act Old*, and the cocreator of the popular baby name website *Nameberry*. A columnist for the *Observer* and for *Glamour* magazine, her *30 Things Every Woman Should Have and Should Know By The Time She's 30* was a viral sensation otherwise known as Maya Angelou's Best Poem Ever. The mother of three grown children, Satran recently moved from New Jersey to Los Angeles.

If you have enjoyed this book
or it has touched your life in some way,
we would love to hear from you.

Please send your comments to:
Hallmark Book Feedback
P.O. Box 419034
Mail Drop 100
Kansas City, MO 64141

Or e-mail us at:
booknotes@hallmark.com